KT-161-704

Gardening

with Children

Collins

Gardening
with Children

Kim Wilde

For H, h and r

First published in 2005 by Collins
an imprint of HarperCollins*Publishers* Ltd
77–85 Fulham Palace Road
London, W6 8JB

The Collins website address is:
www.collins.co.uk

Collins is a registered trademark of
HarperCollins*Publishers* Ltd

Text © 2005 Wildeflower Ltd
Editorial, photography and design © 2005 HarperCollins*Publishers* Ltd
Illustrations © 2005 Judith Glover

Photography: Nikki English
Illustrations: Judith Glover

Editor: Emma Callery
Designer: Bob Vickers

Senior managing editor: Angela Newton
Assistant editor: Lisa John
Design: Luke Griffin
Cover design: Sarah Christie
Production: Chris Gurney

A CIP catalogue record for this book is available from the British Library.

ISBN 0 00 7193114

Colour reproduction by Colourscan
Printed and bound in Great Britain by The Bath Press Ltd

Contents

Gardening with children 25

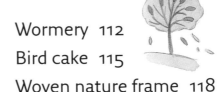

'I particularly enjoyed making the living willow den. I am glad it will be there forever.'
Bryony, age 8

'I really enjoyed making everything in this book and I hope all the projects will introduce more children to gardening.'
Darcey, age 11

'I liked holding the worms best.'
Luke, age 6

'I enjoyed everything I did, but most of all making the wormery.' **Holly, age 8**

'I liked planting the rainbow. I like purple ... that's my favourite colour. When I grow up, I want to be a planter like mummy.' **Rose, age 4**

'I liked the chocolate smell on the plant ... delicious!' **Harry, age 6**

Introduction

In 1996, Hal and I were married and keen to start a family right away. My immediate priority was to create a garden for these yet unborn children, but at the time I had very little experience in gardening, and none in design. I knew I wanted to grow vegetables so that the children would be able to see them grow from seed and they would pick and eat them fresh from the garden. More importantly, I wanted to inspire and delight all of their senses and, with this dream of our own Eden, I took my first steps into the world of horticulture.

Our blank canvas is now brimming over with plants that not only smell and look good, but sound, taste and feel good, too, and the children love to explore and discover all the secrets of the garden for themselves. Keeping a camera handy in the kitchen has encouraged me to keep a record of precious moments such as Harry raiding the raspberry patch, or groaning under the weight of an autumn pumpkin. I have photographs of Harry and Rose as toddlers inquisitively rubbing the lavender plants that crowd the front of our home, or tenderly touching snowdrops I've planted in pots just outside the kitchen.

Encouraging our children to appreciate the natural world around them is a wonderful way to stimulate and excite them, as well as educate them. It is also a marvellous way of spending time with your children, getting to know them, sharing quality time. Gardening with children is also an extremely good way of getting us adults to take time out from busy lives to reconnect with the natural world; perhaps you've never planted a seed yourself. Schools too can benefit from linking gardening projects with the National Curriculum with support from organisations such as the RHS (Royal Horticultural Society) and the organic organisation HDRA (Henry Doubleday Research Association).

I believe that fostering a love of gardening in children is a cumulative thing, built from a collection of small precious moments. If the children see your interest in the garden, their curiosity is automatically ignited, and with your encouragement and enthusiasm they'll be running around searching for ladybirds instead of reaching for the latest DVD. Children's health and obesity issues are of great concern these days; there has never been a stronger argument for encouraging them out into the garden and away from the television. In this book I share with you some of my own garden-inspired experiences with both my own children, and some very special friends. Their enthusiasm for the projects we did together only confirmed what I already knew, that with a little guidance, gardening for children is a natural.

Fun in the garden

The formative years of a child's life are when their minds are wide open, ready to soak up information like a sponge. Their extraordinary and innate **curiosity** leads them to want to know more and, as adults, we are in the privileged position of being able to instil in them an appreciation of the **beautiful**, though troubled, world in which we live. With the dominance of video games, television watching and, of course, homework, I believe that children's opportunities to engage in creative play has never been more compromised.

Creative play forms the foundation of emotional, creative and intellectual growth in later years, but its importance is often misunderstood. By sharing experiences with our children we can help them to develop their own sense of who they are and what their opinions are, as well as establishing that vital **connection** between parent and child. I believe there is no more natural a place to do this than in our own back yards, whether that is a small balcony or a lawn-covered garden. Children love creative play, whether it is cooking, painting, role playing or gardening, and the trick is to be prepared. Invest in some children's **gardening tools,** special children's seed packets (available at good garden centres), and a funky pair of **wellies.** In fact, use anything that makes them feel encouraged and supported.

Encouraging enthusiasm

Gardening requires a certain amount of patience (after all, seeds don't grow into plants overnight), and so most children's love of gardening will be a gradual thing. But there are plenty of ways to start seducing them outside, even if it is only to dig for worms or fill pots full of compost and bedding plants. Children will love watering the pots while beginning to understand what plants need to make them grow. Children also love to do things with you and, while sometimes this is the least help you could want, this is where it pays to be prepared (I knew my time in the Guides would come in useful one day!).

By giving them their own pots, or even a small plot of land, children can gain a sense of responsibility for their efforts, while gaining confidence and knowledge (meanwhile, you can get on with weeding the carrots!). Raised beds are a great idea, especially for children, as they are easier to reach into. Furthermore, because the soil is elevated above ground level it allows the sun to warm it up faster, which means you can plant earlier with better seed germination results. Drainage is improved too, especially as there is no need to tread on the soil and therefore compact it. Again, this will encourage plants to grow better. You can also control the quality of the soil by providing the best compost and organic matter for optimum growth.

Try to locate all gardening projects within sight of the house so that you can keep an eye on what's going on. At the same time, the children will then be better able to monitor their plants' progress.

Making it fun

Encourage children to collect natural objects to draw or use later for craft projects. We keep a tray in the shed for seed heads, feathers, pinecones and snail shells, which always come in handy (see pages 118 and 120). Simple autumn tasks, such as collecting leaves, can be fun, especially for those children with a thing for tidying up (I don't know where Rose gets it from!). It also teaches them the value of recycling organic matter for a healthy garden.

If you don't have a garden, there are plenty of ways to encourage a love of plants for inside, too, such as growing a variety of houseplants from pips or stones from fruit (see page 51). You could also consider growing mustard and cress seeds, which can literally grow overnight on damp kitchen paper. Carrot, turnip, parsnip and radish tops will grow leaves in a saucer with a small amount of water if left on the windowsill, while broad bean, runner bean or pea seeds put into a jar with a damp dishcloth and small amount of water will soon sprout – a great way for children to see how seeds germinate.

Safety in the garden

My brother and I were brought up in a beautiful garden filled with plants that the previous owner had lovingly placed. Unknown to my parents, many of the plants were potentially harmful, and I'm sure if my mum had known, she would have gone around ripping them all out without delay! Luckily she didn't, and Ricky and I grew up surrounded by these lovely plants with no adverse effect. Foxglove, laburnum and wisteria were among the plants that enchanted us, all lovely ... all poisonous! It is important when reading through lists of potentially dangerous plants not to over-react, while at the same time making a considered assessment of any potential danger that might be in your garden. I removed a small laburnum tree from my newly-bought home in 1990, and would not recommend the tree for gardens where young children play, even though both my brother and I survived intact! Besides, there are plenty of other ornamental trees to choose from that offer beautiful blossom, fruit and autumn colour such as many of the *Sorbus* and apple (*Malus*) species.

Take time to acquaint yourself with plants in your garden so that you can show your child plants to avoid as well as those that are quite safe to touch and, of course, instil in them that anything not recognised obviously as food should never be eaten. Wild mushrooms can look just as edible as the ones from the supermarket, but most of them are extremely poisonous and can emerge overnight if the conditions are humid and temperatures moderate. My little girl Rose became concerned in the garden just a few weeks ago as she had touched the foliage of some rhubarb, knowing I'd told her not to because of the poisonous leaves. We simply went into the kitchen and washed her hands, and I suspect she won't do that again in a hurry. It must be said that serious poisoning by plants is rare, but in the event that you think a child has eaten something doubtful, never try to make him or her sick, but take your child straight away to the nearest hospital's Accident and Emergency Department, preferably taking a sample of the offending plant with you.

All children react differently to words of warning, some will take note, others will see it like a red rag to a bull. My advice to anyone concerned about plants is ... if in doubt, pull it out!

Trees and shrubs to be aware of

Berberis darwinii. This dense, evergreen shrub is often used as a hedge but has vicious spines on the stem.

x *Cupressocyparis leylandii* (Leyland cypress). The branches are a skin irritant.

Daphne mezereum. The berries of all species are poisonous. The fragrant pink flowers on bare stems become shiny red berries in summer and look good enough to eat.

Laburnum anagyroides. Long pendulous clusters of yellow flowers cover these fast growing, deciduous trees. All parts of the tree are extremely poisonous, the green, pea-like seed pods could attract young children.

Prunus laurocerasus (cherry laurel). The cherry-like fruits could easily be mistaken for the real thing by a child, but are poisonous.

Prunus lusitanica (Portugal laurel). All parts of the plant contain hydrogen cyanide so on no account should the foliage be burned.

Prunus spinosa (blackthorn). Very long and sharp thorns crowd this native hedgerow species.

Pyracantha. Another tough evergreen with spring flowers and autumn fruit, but sharp thorns could do some damage if a child fell into them.

Ruta graveolens (rue). This shrub is both poisonous and a severe skin irritant.

Taxus baccata. Every part of this slow growing, evergreen plant is poisonous, including dead branches, apart from the pulp around the seed. Grazing animals are particularly vulnerable, becoming sick or dying as a result of consuming it.

Herbaceous plants to be aware of

Aconitum (monkshood). All species and all parts of the plant are very poisonous, especially the root.

Convallaria majalis (lily-of-the-valley). All parts are poisonous.

Delphinium. All parts are toxic.

Digitalis (foxglove). All parts of this beautiful woodland plant are poisonous.

Euphorbia spp. Contains a milky white sap that is toxic and irritates the skin.

Narcissus (daffodil). Bulbs and flowers should not be eaten.

Nicotiana (tobacco plant). All parts are toxic.

Phoradendron flavescens (mistletoe). Berries are toxic.

Rheum raponticum (rhubarb). Leaves are toxic.

Ricinus communis (castor oil plant). This stunning annual has become increasingly popular, especially for those styling a tropical theme in the garden. It is also extremely poisonous. Castor oil plant is more toxic than any other to humans – only one or two of the seeds are a lethal dose.

Tools

Garden tools are often left lying around the garden after use, with your every good intention of putting them away later. When children are in the garden, some of these tools can potentially be extremely dangerous, so always make a habit of putting them away straight after using them and, of course, out of the reach of inquisitive hands! A shed can look very inviting to small people who simply see it as a rather nice Wendy House. To keep young children out, place a bolt at the top of the shed door.

Use some brightly coloured tape to wrap around handles of garden implements as these often have a habit of disappearing. This will help you find them, too, as well as reminding you to put them out of trouble's way. Providing children with their own gardening tools is a great way to motivate them; there are plenty available now in good garden centres, making gardening safer and more fun.

Chemicals

The safest option, and by far the best for your children and garden, is not to have any chemicals at all. There are very effective organic methods and ways of providing safe solutions to garden problems without having to resort to them. Investing in your soil by adding organic matter, such as compost, will help promote healthy soil conditions and healthy plants are far less susceptible to disease. Encouraging beneficial wildlife into the garden can also help keep pests from becoming a problem. Ladybirds, lacewings and hoverflies will feast on aphids while frogs, toads, birds and hedgehogs will gladly go to work on the slugs. If, however, any chemicals are about, of course always put them safely out of harm's way.

Health

Always clear up any cat or dog mess in the garden. Cats especially, can contaminate the soil with their faeces through a disease called toxoplasmosis, which is dangerous to pregnant mums, causing birth defects in the developing baby. Sandpits, too, are a great favourite with the neighbours' cats, even if you don't have your own, so always keep them covered when they aren't in use. Teach your children always to wash their hands after they've been mucking about with soil, and while in the garden encourage them to keep their hands out of their mouths such as when nail biting or sucking thumbs. Soil can also carry tetanus, so check with your doctor if you're not sure whether the tetanus vaccinations are up to date for both you and your child.

Always make sure the children wear hats, long-sleeved T-shirts and sun cream in sunny weather, and always avoid the sun around the middle part of the day. It is estimated that we get about 80 per cent of our total lifetime sun exposure in the first 18 years of our lives, so clearly protection in childhood is very important in order to prevent skin cancer in later life. Use sunscreens that block both UVA and UVB light with a minimum sun protection factor (SPF) 15, and always buy it fresh each summer as sunscreen does expire.

Water

Never let young children out of your site if there is water ANYWHERE in the garden. It only takes a few centimetres to cause death by drowning and can happen in the most innocuous circumstances. One of my own experiences scared me so much that I removed the very large pond in our garden, even though the incident had nothing to do with it. While gardening with Harry (a toddler at the time),

I felt safe in the knowledge that the pond was securely fenced off, so was fairly relaxed about him mooching around while I weeded. Fortunately, John our gardener noticed that Harry had balanced himself somewhat precariously over the edge of a plastic container, which had collected a small amount of rain. He was having trouble getting his feet back down to the ground and could easily have tipped forwards into the plastic container. Unable to find the strength to push himself out of the water, he could have drowned in a split second. I still feel extremely sick just thinking about it.

Climbing areas

Areas where children are likely to fall need to have some kind of impact absorbing surface such as bark chips (which we've used a lot), or a more expensive synthetic plastic or rubber matting. Bark chips used for this purpose need to be at a depth of 25cm (10in), and checked regularly to make sure that this depth is maintained. Grass, dirt and concrete won't provide any protection at all. Avoid sand in play areas as it can get in children's eyes, noses and ears, and also attracts animals that will use it as a toilet. Also, always check for sharp angles, hooks, splinters or any protrusions that could catch on children's clothing. Avoid using decking in shady areas as they become like ice rinks in wet conditions. If you do want to use decking, choose a ridged decking product, which definitely helps overcome the problem.

Security

- Check that gates fasten securely so that even if a child should find a chair to reach it, they still couldn't unlock it.
- Gaps in the fence or garden boundary will soon be discovered by inquisitive children and should be made secure; neighbours may well have a pond you don't know about or an unfriendly animal.
- Protect the ends of bamboo canes and other sticks in the ground with little stoppers, in case of accidental damage to passing small people.
- Check, too, that if you hold a summer party in the garden, glasses aren't left lying around. They might break, which could result in a cut foot.

Garden basics

Sowing seeds

Growing plants from seed is very rewarding as well as being economical – I saw pumpkins the other day selling for what it would cost to grow a hundred!

Always follow the instructions on the back of the packet; some seeds germinate in darkness while others need a bright windowsill, and many seeds can be sown directly into the open ground.

Use **multipurpose compost** or special seed compost for sowing seeds in seed trays or pots.

Always **sow seeds sparsely** so there is less thinning to do. This produces healthy, sturdy seedlings. Seeds sown too densely will become straggly and weak.

Sow seeds on lightly firmed compost that is slightly damp and sow them to the depth stated on the packet. Cover with compost, and gently firm.

Water seeds with a fine water spray so as not to disturb them. Don't use very cold water on very young plants – tepid is preferable, so as not to shock them!

Looking after seedlings

By covering seed trays or pots with cling film you can reduce the likelihood of the compost drying out while seeds are germinating. The film will also help to keep in heat, but do always check to make sure the compost doesn't dry out.

Unless stated otherwise, put **trays and pots** somewhere warm and sunny until they have germinated.

As soon as you see a seed sprouting, **remove** the cling film from over the top of the pots.

When seedlings are **large enough** to handle they need pricking out to give them more room to grow. You can use a pencil for this. Water them well before pricking out, to minimise root damage.

Re-pot into pots or trays of fresh compost, and water gently – don't forget to label your plants!

In late spring, when there are **no more frosts,** you can put seedlings outside for a few hours each day to prepare them for being planted in the garden. This is called hardening off.

Transplanting seedlings

Before planting, always weed and prepare the ground by removing big stones and raking until the surface is even.

Always handle young plants **gently** when transferring them to their final growing position. Give them a good soaking with water and then transfer plants from small pots by gently tapping the bottom of a tilted pot.

Make a hole large enough for each plant and position at the same level they were in when in the pot. Add some water to the hole.

Push soil gently around the plant and water again.

If growing plants in **containers,** make sure there are drainage holes at the base of the container. Add a layer of crocks (broken flower pots), small stones, gravel or broken up pieces of polystyrene before adding the compost.

Leave a **small space** at the top of the container so that when you water it doesn't all spill over.

Making life easier

Consider using slow-release fertiliser tablets and water retaining granules for low maintenance.

If planting in several containers, consider grouping them all together so that watering is easier.

Some plants, such as the sunflowers on page 26, need some support or they'll flop over. Bamboo canes and garden twine tied loosely will do the job. Peas can be grown through twiggy branches.

Gardening
with children

Sunflower bed

AGE RANGE **Three years onwards**

TIME OF YEAR **Late spring**

Collection of 2 litre fizzy drink bottles

Packet of sunflower seeds: don't forget them!

Tall stake, e.g. bamboo pole

Garden twine

The large seeds of sunflowers (*Helianthus annuus*) are easy for children to handle and simple to grow. With *Jack and the Beanstalk*-like proportions, these hardy annuals will germinate, grow, flower and set seed in one growing season (usually between March and October). We are growing them in the ground, but they can easily be planted in large pots or containers filled with multipurpose compost – as long as you don't forget to water them.

Sunflowers come in a wide variety of sizes ranging from 60cm (2ft) to giant ones, which can reach an incredible 5m (15ft)! You could grow different heights of sunflower in tiers for a chorus of happy sunflower faces, guaranteed to make you all smile. There are also pollen-free varieties for hay fever sufferers, such as 'Double Shine F1 Hybrid', which grow to 1.5m (5ft) high.

To deter slugs from devouring your small seedlings as they emerge, as well as helping to keep seeds warm and moist, cut large 2 litre plastic lemonade bottles in half. Place the top half of the bottles over the seeds once they are planted (see opposite). Don't forget to take the tops off for ventilation and also for watering.

Clear the bed of large stones in late April. Sunflowers can be grown in any soil but will thrive in soil that is rich and well-drained.

Insert **individual seeds** 2cm (1in) deep and about 15cm (6in) apart (distance depends on the variety, you might have to plant giant ones up to 40cm (16in) apart). Cover with lemonade bottle cloches (described opposite). Seedlings should appear within 14 days and then flower about 45 days later. Remove the cloches when the seedlings are well established.

Water daily to keep the seeds moist until well established and keep watering them regularly thereafter.

If plants are appearing to become over-crowded, carefully dig some out and re-plant immediately.

A stake such as **a bamboo pole** will help to support taller varieties. Tie the sunflower to the cane with a soft garden twine.

Flowering will begin in June and continue through to October. To get the best from your seeds, see the advice overleaf.

Getting the best from your seeds

Sunflower seeds can be sown outdoors where they are to grow from late April to May. Plant seedlings started earlier (March to April) indoors in their flowering positions 60cm (24in) apart from May onwards after the last frost.

If sowing indoors, sow seeds individually in small pots filled with moist seed compost and lightly cover the seeds. Accustom plants to outside conditions a few weeks before planting out in May.

Choose a sunny spot (they are, however, surprisingly tolerant of partial shade) for sowing your seeds or transplanting the pots, trying to plant them facing the sun – you don't want to end up with their backs to you!

Water them regularly.
Adding a high nitrogen liquid feed every two weeks or so will help your sunflowers to flourish, but is not always necessary.

Enjoy your sunflowers

- Why not have a competition to see who can grow the tallest sunflower? (Parents: get handy with the liquid feed!)
- Encourage your children to do sunflower paintings, perhaps show them Van Gogh's famous masterpieces for inspiration.
- Roast the seeds for 40 minutes in the oven until brown and crispy. Then sprinkle with soy sauce for a delicious and nutritious snack, or eat them raw.

Flower power

Annual seeds of flowers or vegetables in a tape are available from good garden centres, and are ideal for the youngest hands as they are so easy to handle. Bold, simple motfis work really well for this project, such as letters from the alphabet. Children can learn to write their own names from three years old, so can easily do this project from that age with just a little help. Our 'seeds in a tape' were cornflower (*Centaurea cyanus*) 'Polka Dot mix', which are a mixture of double-flowered dwarf varieties of cornflowers in shades of blue, pink, carmine and white reaching 40cm (16in). Cornflowers are hardy annuals, which means they can be safely sown

outside when the soil has started to warm up in early spring, ready to flower in the summer.

Other hardy annuals you could choose include candytuft (*Iberis umbellata*), love-in-a-mist (*Nigella damascena*), poached egg plant (*Limnanthes douglasii*) and pot marigold (*Calendula officinalis*).

Sow seeds from March to May and choose a sunny, well-drained, weed-free position. Some seeds, such as pot marigold, cornflower and poached egg plants, can be sown outdoors in the autumn to produce flowers the following spring.

Make a channel in the soil about 13mm (½in) deep, and place the tape into whatever shape you've decided on.

Cover the tape lightly with soil and water well. Soon you'll see tiny young plants growing. As they grow bigger, remove some of the young plants so they are 15–23cm (6–9in) apart to give them room to grow.

Pick out any weeds, and keep watered in dry weather.

Ivy heart

AGE RANGE **Four years onwards**
TIME OF YEAR **Spring–winter**

Wire coat hanger
Small-leaved common ivy
(*Hedera helix*); we chose one with
plenty of trailing growth for an instant
effect, but you could buy a smaller one
and train it over time
Soil-based potting compost
Container (we used a stylish but
simple terracotta pot), with crocks at
the base for drainage

When gardening with children, always be guided by their personality and mood. For instance, planting seeds can quickly turn into a free-for-all, and end up with them mucking about with the earth, all planting of seeds forgotten! Some days it is better just to be grateful they're outside at all, surrounded by nature and away from the video or DVD player. Quick fixes have their place where children are concerned, just as they sometimes do for us big kids, and this little project will only take a matter of minutes. It easily keeps the attention of the most distracted child and produces a charming, natural sculpture that lasts.

Take the wire coat hanger and bend into the shape of a heart.

Plant the ivy in the container with crocks in the base for drainage. First add soil-based potting compost to the bottom of the container and then around the ivy to keep it firmly in place.

Insert the coat hanger in a central position in the pot and feed the ivy around the wire shape.

Before you know it, you have a **living heart.** Water the compost regularly, tucking in new growth and trimming occasionally.

Other things to do

There are all kinds of ready-made wire frames available from garden centres including ducks, rabbits and cats.

A liquid feed every two weeks will give you a happy heart!

You could always underplant your ivy heart with pretty summer bedding plants, or low growing plants such as *Sempervivum* or ornamental cabbage, as we have (see opposite).

Ivy dinosaur

AGE RANGE **Four years onwards**

TIME OF YEAR **Spring–winter**

Plastic coated wire

Container, with crocks at the base
for drainage

Soil-based potting compost

Small-leaved common ivy
(*Hedera helix*) (see page 30)

Few subjects in the world are as fascinating to the public as dinosaurs, and it is amazing to think that they roamed this planet over 230 million years ago, and then mysteriously disappeared 65 million years ago. My children love dinosaurs – well, at least the cuddly ones with American accents!

Like the Ivy heart project (see page 30), this idea takes very little time (less than half an hour), and is suitable for children aged from four years upwards.

Cut off 2m (6ft 6in) of the plastic-coated wire, create a hoop and then twist the ends together.

Squeeze the wire hoop into shape, making a tail, a humped body, a long neck and head, not forgetting to twist the ends together for about 15cm (6in) to stick into the soil.

Fill your chosen container with soil-based compost and position the dinosaur frame in it.

Plant the ivy at the base of the dinosaur frame, ensuring both are firmly in place, and wrap the leaves around the wire.

Underplant a selection of houseleeks (*Sempervivum*) and small-leaved stonecrop (*Sedum*) varieties to give a really prehistoric look.

As it grows, continue to **feed the ivy** around the wire shape, trimming it as necessary. Water regularly and give the ivy a fortnightly liquid feed to keep it in tip-top condition.

Underplanting

Suitable *Sempervivum* varieties include: *Sempervivum tectorum* and *S. arachnoideum*.
Suitable *Sedum* varieties include: *Sedum acre*, *S. spathuifolium* 'Purpurium' and *S. spurium*.

Rose's rainbow

Some sticks cut to the same length for markers

String

Annual seeds

Ribbon in each colour of the rainbow or lots of string

Multipurpose compose for spare seeds

We have planted our rainbow with annuals, which are seeds that complete their life cycle in one year – growing from seed, flowering, setting seed and then dying – making them ideal for keeping children's interest. Although a rainbow has seven colours – red, orange, yellow, green, blue, indigo and violet – we have planted six, missing out indigo as it is so similar to blue. You don't have to make a rainbow; you could do any pattern you like, perhaps a name, a flag or a favourite painting.

To help motivate the children even more, we marked out the rainbow using coloured ribbon so there is something colourful to enjoy while waiting for the annuals to flower later in the summer. Of course, string will do if there's no ribbon to hand.

Choose a sunny spot in the

garden (we have used a raised vegetable bed), and dig and rake the soil until it is fine and crumbly on top. Take extra care to eradicate all weeds and large stones.

Mark out an area for your rainbow. To do this, at the base of the rainbow,

measure along half way and place a stick marker.

To form your first rainbow arc,

tie a length of string to the first stick marker and tie a second stick at the point where the innermost arc will start. Pull the string tight across the soil and score a semi-circle with the second stick.

Place more stick markers

at regular points along the scored line so the arc's outline is clearly marked out. To help ensure the markers are evenly spaced, use a short piece of stick as a measuring gauge between each marker. Repeat for each arc of the rainbow. As your arcs become larger, you might have space for less of the outline, depending on the size of your bed.

Tie each coloured ribbon (we started with the

shortest circle, violet) to the first marker of each arc and feed the ribbon around the rest of the markers in the semi-circle. Repeat with the next colour (blue) and so on, ending with red at the outside edge.

Sow the seeds,

making sure you read the sowing instructions. Most seeds should be about 6mm (¼in) below the surface, although others may need to be deeper.

Water with a fine spray,

and keep watering regularly thereafter.

Keep an eye on weeds,

which will love these ideal growing conditions. Perhaps sow a few of each of the seeds in small pots of multipurpose compost to help you recognise flowers from weeds.

When the seedlings appear

you may need to remove some carefully to make sure they have plenty of room to grow.

Choosing your plants

Buy annuals that flower at about the same time and have similar heights. We have used:
For red: scarlet flax (*Linum*)
For orange: pot marigold (*Calendula officinalis*)
For yellow: beach evening primrose (*Camissonia cheiranthifolia*)
For green: marjoram (*Origanum vulgare*)
For blue: *Legousia* 'Blue Carpet'
For violet: swan river daisy (*Brachyscome*)
These annuals can be sown outdoors April–May.

Other annuals that are easy to grow include:
Cornflower *(Centaurea)*. These come in blue, purple, pink rose and white.
Poached egg plant *(Limnanthes douglasii)*. This pretty annual has fresh green foliage and (you've guessed it) flowers that resemble a poached egg!
Zinnia. Colours include vivid scarlet and yellow.

Alternatively, you can find lots of annuals in garden centres as ready-to-grow plants.

Calendula officinalis

Centaurea cyanus

Scarecrows

AGE RANGE **Six years onwards**

TIME OF YEAR **Spring–autumn**

Two sturdy bamboo canes

Ball of strong garden twine

Old pair of tights

Old clothes, including a front-opening top, trousers, old garden gloves and a hat (we raided Rose and Harry's dressing-up box)

Straw to stuff the tights and gloves

Old football or plastic flowerpot for a head (at last, a use for an old, deflated football!)

Exterior paint for covering the head and adding features

Bottle tops for eyes

Old party hat for the nose

Good strong glue

Adult with a drill, to make a hole in the football

Plastic flowerpot for a hat

Old garden gloves for hands

The sight of a scarecrow far away in the middle of a field has always held a fascination for me. It delights me when farmers still use them, and – although rare – you'll occasionally see one that distracts the eye and, for the briefest of moments, you're tricked ... just like the crows!

Making your own scarecrow starts with the construction of the basic cross framework, which you can dress and then take it from there. Children would be able to help with the tying and gluing, but the project will need adult supervision. A few pairs of hands are helpful in the construction. Remember that the sturdier you make your scarecrow, the better, as wind and rain will soon batter it – not to mention the attention of the children (mine took to cuddling theirs!).

We placed our scarecrows in the raspberries, where they've done a pretty good job at entertaining the children, and seeing off any unwanted visitors. Of course, there are no hard and fast rules about scarecrow making, so have fun re-inventing this most ancient of rituals.

Stand one of the bamboo canes upright with the thickest end pointing down, to form the base of the scarecrow.

Tie the shorter cane to it to form a cross. Use the garden twine and have the horizontal cane at arm height. Make sure this framework is sturdy enough to withstand the elements, birds and children!

Fill old tights with straw to form the legs and then tie them to the bamboo cross.

Attach the clothes. A front-opening shirt is easier to get on but, of course, a princess dress can be just slipped over.

Tie the trousers over the tights. We looped the twine over the arms when tying for extra security.

Make your head from an old flowerpot or football (see overleaf) and then attach to the clothed frame.

Fill old garden gloves with straw and tie onto each arm.

Flowerpot head

With the bottom of the pot as the top of the head, glue on bottle tops for eyes.

Cut down an old party hat for the nose, re-attach the elastic to the nose part of the hat and slide over the flowerpot. Then paint on a mouth.

Hold the head against the cane and ask an adult to cut off any excess bamboo. Place the flowerpot on the cane – we found one of the holes in the flowerpot was the same size as the cane, which helped keep it secure.

On with the hat!

Football head

Get an adult to drill a hole in the old football and then paint the football in whatever colour you like (we used outdoor water-based paint, which is weather-resistant and child safe). Leave to dry.

Glue on bottle tops for the eyes and nose. Then glue on the flowerpot hat and leave to dry.

Cut the cane as for the flowerpot head and then slide the football over the cane and, finally, paint on the mouth.

Willow den

AGE RANGE **Eight years onwards**

TIME OF YEAR **Spring–summer**

Bundles of living willow

Black maul willow for added strength and windows

Marker sticks

String

Spade and spike for lifting turf and making holes

Bark chippings

Compost

Biodegradable twine

The best time to plant a living willow structure is between the beginning of February and the end of April when early spring rains help the roots to establish. Living willow is so versatile it can be used in all sorts of ways; I've seen it make fantastic tunnels, rustic arbours, leafy fences and beautiful sculptures.

We have used three different kinds of willow. The main den was planted with hybrid red (*Salix caprea, cinera, viminalis, caladendron*), which has velvety red stems. The diagonals were planted with cane osier (*Salix viminalis*), which has contrasting yellow-green stems. The willow used for non-living weaving was black maul (*Salix triandra*).

Willow is sold in bundles or 'wads', and it is essential to keep all living willow rods in water to ensure they will take root when planted.

Mark out the den area by creating a perfect circle – ours has a diameter of 2m (6ft). To do this, place a marker in the ground at the centre of what will be the den. Tie a piece of string to it (in our case, 1m (3ft) long) and pull taut. Attach a small stick at the other end to begin marking the perimeter of the den.

Use **small sticks** of willow to mark the outline. Once complete, lift the turf to reveal the soil beneath.

Cover the soil with bark chippings, leaving a small trench of soil all around the outside (this is where you will be planting the willow rods).

With a spike, **make holes** about 30cm (12in) deep and 20cm (8in) apart, depending on whether your desired feature is going to be closely woven or open. We used a small piece of willow stick to ensure even spacing between each hole.

Fill each hole with compost and then water. The idea is to make the hole as saturated as possible, ready for the willow.

At the entrance to the den, make three or four holes close together on either side so that several rods can eventually be gathered together to make a really sturdy opening.

Now you are ready to **start planting** the hybrid red rods. Using secateurs, cut the base end of the willow rod at a diagonal, then insert the long willow stem into each hole, holding it firmly near the base while packing in more compost.

Work around the den circle until you have willow outlining the whole shape.

Work out the height of the doorway by getting the largest child to stand by the frame. Of course, this doesn't exclude us big kids!

Twist and tie together the closely planted willow stems that are to make the door arch. Doorways in children's play features need the strength of several rods planted together.

Plant diagonal stems (the cane osier) in exactly the same way as the first circle, forming an outer circle. We positioned the stems between the vertical rods. Diagonal planting adds strength to the structure and the shoots, which grow vertically from the diagonal rod, enclosing the den.

Weave the diagonal stems across the vertical rods making sure you weave them in both directions for added strength.

At the same time, **weave horizontal pieces** of black maul around the den at about the top of the door height to give added strength. We stopped weaving our diagonal stems at this height.

To make windows, we used the black maul to create circles, which we positioned at the children's head height. We tied them into the structure with biodegradable twine, as well as weaving them in using black maul.

Use long pieces of black maul to **draw together** the top of the vertical stems so the den is enclosed. A circle of black maul woven over the den towards the top helps give it strength.

Keep your den well watered throughout the summer until the willow is established.

Living willow

Willow is tolerant of most soil types and flourishes in water-retentive, clay soil. The willows I've used do not have an invasive root system, but take care not to plant too near to buildings or drains. During the growing season, weave in new growth and trim and shape when dormant in winter or early spring. Plant annuals such as sweet peas (*Lathyrus odoratus*), poppies (*Papaver*) or climbing nasturtiums (*Tropaeolum*) at the base of the circle to add colour and fragrance.

Remember, planting with living willow is not an exact science; it doesn't matter if it's not perfect. You'll find out very quickly how best to work with the willow, so don't be scared of having a go!

Star wands

Star and heart wands are easy and fun to make and are the ideal way of using up leftover stems from the willow den, or any other living willow construction you have made for your garden.

These wands look lovely placed among flowers in the border, and can be useful to mark out places to remind you where bulbs are planted. We stuck some of our wands in the ground – and they took root and produced pretty leaves! We also made a large star wand and attached it to the top of the den.

Take a small piece of black maul (*Salix triandra*) willow stem and, towards the thinnest end, bend the willow into the shape of an 'M'.

Turn the 'M' into **two triangles** that overlap each other so that three points of the star have been created. To make the fourth point, take the end of the stem through the largest triangle.

Create the fifth and final point of the star by once more taking the end of the stem back through the star. To finish off, twist the thin end around the main stem.

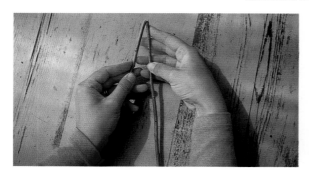

Heart wands

The heart wands are slightly easier to make than the stars, and look charming decorating containers or stuck in a scarecrow's hat. We also made willow noughts and crosses and some long-legged birds!

Green willow is freshly cut and is ideal for finer weaving and supple enough to weave without soaking. It remains flexible for up to six weeks. If you have ordered some bundles and are storing them, cut the bundles open to allow air to circulate and store in a cool shady place. Once dried it is known as 'brown' willow and will need pre-soaking for five to seven days before using.

Take a flexible stem of black maul and make one bend about three-quarters from the base of the stem to form the bottom point of the heart.

Then it is simply a matter of bending the top part of the stem into half the heart shape on one side, and again on the other side.

Tie the thin end of the willow onto the main stem around the base of the heart.

Courgettes

AGE RANGE **Four years onwards**

TIME OF YEAR **Spring-summer**

5-7.5cm (2-3in) pots
Multipurpose compost
Courgette seeds
Tomato fertiliser

Courgettes are relatively fast growing vegetables, so are ideal for children. They also taste great and can be grated raw into sandwiches with carrot for a healthy, nutritious snack. The flowers, too, are edible and can be dipped in batter and fried, or stuffed with rice, peppers, onion and garlic. Growing vegetables in containers is a good option for those with little space, or for children, who can see them growing right under their noses!

Plenty of water is essential, especially when the plant is in flower, and, of course, as the fruits start to swell. Water-retaining gel crystals are a great way to help keep containers from drying out, especially during the summer, and can be added before planting. You could also add some slow-release fertiliser granules to provide nutrients throughout the growing period. Always choose large containers as they don't dry out so quickly, and always pay attention to good drainage. Mulching containers helps to retain moisture: use leaf mould, straw, spent mushroom compost or garden compost. Once the plants start to crop, harvest them regularly to stimulate more fruits ... you'll be amazed at how quickly they'll produce more and more courgettes.

Fill individual pots

with multipurpose compost.

The seeds are large and
flat and are best sown on their sides,
pointed end downwards. (If planted
flat, there is a chance that the seeds
can become too wet and rot.) It is also
a good idea to soak the seeds overnight
before sowing them.

Varieties to try

'Ambassador F1' produces bumper crops
of small, dark green fruit with an
excellent flavour.

'Leprechaun' is a decorative variety
producing little round fruit.

'Bambino F1' has dark green baby fruits
over a long period.

Many vegetables can be grown in
containers and the mini-veg varieties are
especially good. These are specially bred or
chosen to be either picked young or grown
closer together than normal size varieties –
and they're very tasty too!

Place one seed in each pot and gently firm in.

Water thoroughly and position on a warm windowsill.
When the plants have developed a few leaves, harden off outside during the day
but bring them back in at night.

Plant out the courgette plants after any threat from frost in a sunny, sheltered spot.

Provide support for trailing varieties by inserting bamboo
canes and/or feeding the stems through trellis. Choose bush or small varieties
when growing courgettes in containers. Pinch out the tips of trailing varieties
when they reach 60cm (2ft) long.

Water well and when the fruits start to swell, feed
them every two weeks with a tomato fertiliser.

Monkey nuts

AGE RANGE   **Four years onwards**
TIME OF YEAR   **Spring-autumn**

Handful of monkey nuts
Small flowerpots
Multipurpose compost
Clear plastic bags

Peanuts, or monkey nuts, are not really nuts at all. Nuts grow on trees, but peanuts grow in the ground and are part of the same family as peas and beans. Peanuts grow into pretty plants with rounded leaves and yellow flowers and are easily grown. A crop of nuts is a bit harder ... but, even so, it is definitely worth having a go!

Plant the nuts in March or April and watch for yellow flowers in summer that turn into brown seed pods. Amazingly, these pods grow down to the soil surface and bury themselves, ready to grow!

Make a slit in the casings of the monkey nuts. This will enable water to get to the seeds inside, and so speed up growth.

Take containers with drainage holes and fill to almost the top with multipurpose compost, then water.

Position the nuts **on the compost,** cover with more compost and water again.

Cover the pots with clear plastic bags and tie the ends. This is to keep the moisture in and prevent the peanuts from drying out. Put the pots in the airing cupboard or another warm place. Check regularly and water to prevent drying out.

When the seeds have sprouted, **remove the plastic bags** and position on a sunny windowsill.

As seedlings develop, **re-pot them** in groups (they like to grow together) in a large pot filled with multipurpose compost. They need a big pot so they have room to bury their seeds.

Water well, and regularly thereafter. There is no need to feed the young plants as this will prevent flowering and therefore nuts.

When in flower, **stand the plants** in the garden so bees can pollinate the flowers. A crop should be ready by autumn when the plant turns yellow and dies. Just pull out the plant and you'll see nuts growing off the roots.

Other pips to grow

Why don't you try to grow other pips such as orange, apple, avocado pear or mango?

Citrus pips need to be soaked for two days, and then like to be grown in sandy compost, so mix sharp sand with multipurpose compost and water well before planting. Spread pips over the surface and cover with 1cm (½in) of the same mixture. Then do as above for monkey nuts by covering with a plastic bag and positioning in a warm place. This also applies to apple pips but, of course, small apple plants are hardy and can be grown outside, although it may take several years for any fruit to grow.

Avocado pears make good houseplants and are quick and easy to grow. Choose a stone from a very ripe avocado and soak it for a few days. Plant the stone in a medium-sized pot with multipurpose compost and always make sure the pot has drainage holes. Soak the container through and plant the stone fat end down with the top only just sticking out of the compost. Then it's back to the plastic bag, airing cupboard and sunny windowsill regime! To keep the plant bushy, nip off the growing tips occasionally and feed during the summer.

Tomatoes

AGE RANGE **Four years onwards**
TIME OF YEAR **Spring–autumn**

Flowerpots, with crocks
at the base for drainage
Multipurpose compost
Tomato seeds
Old sieve
Cling film

We always plant the 'Tumbler' variety, which is a dwarf, trailing tomato specially bred for containers, and place it outside the back door for easy picking. The fruit is produced over a long period and is always deliciously sweet and easy to grow; the small fruit is also perfect for little hands.

Raising plants from seed is very straightforward and rewarding, but if time is tight, don't worry – garden centres always have a good variety of plants in late spring ready to plant up. Grow container plants in good quality multipurpose compost in containers about 30cm (1ft) wide, or simply use grow bags.

Once the plants start to crop, you can encourage growth by giving the plants a liquid tomato feed once a week – tomatoes are hungry plants.

Fill a pot or seed tray with multipurpose compost. Make sure the container has good drainage and crocks in the bottom. Water well, then level and firm the compost.

Sprinkle a few (not too many) of the tomato seeds on the surface and then cover them with a light dusting of sifted compost.

Place the container **somewhere warm** inside, perhaps a windowsill. Covering the container with cling film will help retain moisture and encourage germination, which should take about ten days.

When the **seedlings emerge,** prick them out into individual pots. Do this by using a pencil/dibber, gradually loosening the seedling. Carefully lift the seedling by the leaf not the stem.

Plant each seedling into individual pots and move to a well lit windowsill where plants will grow rapidly.

Keep the plants **well watered,** but take care not to over water. They can be planted outside after any threat of frost in late May.

Getting a good crop

Good tomato varieties for growing outside the house include: 'Moneymaker', 'Gardener's Delight', and 'Tumbling Tom Red'/ 'Tumbling Tom Yellow'.

We planted one to three 'Tumbler' plants per container (depending on its size), and placed them in a sunny, sheltered spot. 'Tumbler' needs no support but other varieties might benefit from a cane inserted in the pot and then the tomato tied in loosely with garden twine. Pinch out the growing tip after four or five pairs of leaves so the plant concentrates all its effort on ripening fruit.

Pumpkins

AGE RANGE **Four years onwards**

TIME OF YEAR **Spring–autumn**

Small pots, with crocks at
the base for drainage

Multipurpose compost

Pumpkin seeds

Well-rotted manure

Garden compost

Halloween wouldn't be the same without a pumpkin, although carving them out is a much longer job than you might think. Having gone down that route a few times, I now carve faces onto a baby pumpkin, and as the pumpkin grows, so does the face. Brilliant! They are very easy to grow, and once planted in the ground they quickly develop flowers and fruit. When the pumpkins are small, children can draw a simple design on several of them. An adult can then trace over the fruits with a knife, breaking the skin. As the pumpkins grow, so will the designs. Our pumpkin has a smile that grows and grows! For an alternative idea, you could try writing names on yours.

In order to thrive, pumpkins need rich soil with lots of well-rotted manure, plenty of sunshine and regular watering. Soaking the seeds in warm water 24 hours before planting will help to speed up germination.

Pumpkin flowers

Most pumpkin plants have separate male (pollen-bearing) and female (seed-bearing) flowers. Sometime in July the plant begins to form flowers; initially these will all be male flowers, the female flowers follow a few weeks later.

I find this really interesting, as most flowers are hermaphrodite – which means they have both male and female parts – but on pumpkin plants you can observe male and female flowers separately. Male flowers are on thin stems about 20cm (4in) above the vine. Female flowers are close to the vine, with a tiny baby pumpkin between the flower and the vine stem. Whether these baby pumpkins develop into full-sized ones depends on the female flowers being pollinated by bees and other insects; if they are not, they will shrivel and die.

To ensure pollination of female flowers, some gardeners take nature into their own hands and pick a male flower and rub the stamen with the pollen onto the stigma of the female flower ... the mind boggles!

Male flower

Female flower

Fill individual pots
with multipurpose compost. Sow the seeds between mid-April and mid-May by first making a small hole with your finger.

Place the pumpkin
seed, one per pot, with pointy side down and on its edge – not on its flat side. Firm over with compost.

Water,
and keep in warm conditions. Initially we placed ours on a sunny windowsill, moving it later to a frost-free greenhouse.

Dig holes
to plant out the pumpkins when the pumpkin plants are established and the last frost is past (usually towards the end of May). If planting several plants, make sure you space the holes 1m (3ft) apart.

Before planting, incorporate plenty of well-rotted **manure** and garden compost to the soil. Pumpkins are heavy feeders.

Pumpkin patch

Carefully put a small baby pumpkin inside a large, square, plastic milk container. As it grows, the pumpkin will fill the space. Cut away the container and you have a pumpkin shaped like a large dice!

Tie a rope around the middle of a young, green pumpkin and, as it grows, it will swell at either end, making the pumpkin look like a Russian doll.

Look out for 'Jack-O-Lantern' varieties, and if you want to grow a REALLY BIG one, choose 'Atlantic Giant' for a chance to grow a record breaker.

Carefully tip
the plant out of the pot, plant it in the hole and firm in.

Keep well watered
– this is essential for a really large pumpkin. Pumpkins are 90 per cent water. A liquid feed every two weeks helps too.

Once the desired numbers of **pumpkins** have formed, pinch out the growing tips. Reducing the number of fruit to one or two per plant will ensure larger fruit. Pinching off the top of the shoots when they reach 60cm (24in) long will make the plant bushy.

Peas

AGE RANGE **Five years onwards**

TIME OF YEAR **Spring–autumn**

Manure

Bamboo canes or other means of support

Garden twine

Willow withies

Pea seeds

One of my favourite summer memories is of Rose and me munching our way through a row of sweet, delicious peas in our vegetable garden. Not only are peas good to eat, they have a beauty all of their own, producing pretty flowers and delicate twining tendrils – and they are packed with vitamins and minerals. Don't leave peas to over mature on the plant as this will slow up pea production dramatically, it's definitely a case of the more you pick, the more peas will be produced.

So that you can be eating fresh garden peas from May until October, plant different varieties; they all take roughly three months to mature from sowing (see below). Peas prefer well dug, rich soil in a sunny, sheltered position; never plant peas in cold, wet soil. If possible, dig in some well-rotted manure in the autumn, which will provide good nutrition for when you sow the first peas in March.

It is perfectly easy to grow peas supported up a wigwam in a container; in just the same way as you would grow sweet pea flowers. All peas will crop much better with some kind of support, whether it is with pea sticks made from hazel brushwood, or bamboo canes like we've used, woven with willow sticks. Supports can be put in before planting or just as the seedlings are emerging and you can plant the peas in single or double rows.

I grow pot marigolds (*Calendula officinalis*) in the vegetable garden, which self-seed everywhere. Not only do they provide a sunny splash of colour, but they also attract beneficial insects such as ladybirds, hoverflies and lacewings into the garden.

Getting the best from your peas

'Feltham First', 'Meteor' and 'Douce Provence' are hardier than other types of peas, and can also be sown directly into the ground from mid-winter to early spring if you can provide cover for seedlings and plants with cloches. Varieties that are suitable for sowing from early spring to summer include 'Kelvedon Wonder', 'Hurst Green Shaft' and 'Sugar Snap', which is a very sweet mangetout type that can be eaten whole.

To help prevent disease, never grow peas in the same spot for more than a year. Once you have finished with the peas, leave the roots in the ground as this helps to improve soil fertility.

Place the bamboo canes in pairs firmly
into the soil about 60cm (2ft) apart.

Bind each pair together about
1.5m (5ft) from the ground with garden twine.

Position a horizontal cane for stability
through the upright canes and bind.

Weave willow withies
between the poles at fairly close intervals for the pea tendrils to cling on to.

Dig a shallow drill 2.5–5cm (1–2in)
deep and drop seeds into damp soil, 5–7.5cm (2–3in) apart. Cover with soil and water.

As the **seedlings** develop,
the tendrils will cling to the support, but any trailing on the ground can be gently helped back on to the support.

Keep the area free from weeds and **water**
occasionally, especially during dry spells.

Strawberry tower

AGE RANGE **Six years onwards**
TIME OF YEAR **Late spring–autumn**
Three containers in different sizes, plus crocks for lining the base
Multipurpose compost
Strawberry plants, about six will do

You know summer has really arrived when the strawberries are ready. Supermarkets are crammed with those impossibly perfect, suspiciously large, artificial-looking strawberries (*Fragaria* x *ananassa*) that inevitably don't taste that great, and goodness knows what process they went through to get them to look like that. Growing your own strawberries is a much better option as you know exactly what's gone into them, and growing them in containers means that the fruit is kept off the soil and it is easier to keep slugs away from your juicy produce.

Over-watering is the most common reason that strawberry plants fail, so be sure not to let the soil become saturated. The nutrients in fresh compost should be sufficient to provide good growth until the plants flower; thereafter, give a weekly liquid feed high in potash and low in nitrates (e.g. tomato fertiliser) until the fruit starts turning colour. From June on, the plants start producing stolons, on which runners will form – cut these off as soon as they appear, to encourage the plant to keep producing fruit.

By choosing different varieties – see opposite – it is possible to enjoy your own strawberries from late May until the autumn frosts.

Line the largest pot with crocks and fill with multipurpose compost. Repeat with the other two and give them all a good watering.

Stack the pots, one on top of the other.

Take individual **strawberry plants** and plant them up. Make sure the crown – the point at which roots and leaves join – is just above the level of the soil. Firm the plants in.

Site in **a sunny, sheltered position** and water regularly. As the plants grow, they should spill over the edges to create a cascade effect.

Always water strawberry plants close to the crown. Hosepipe spraying will encourage disease, and wet fruits can develop a fungal disease called botrytis.

Choose your variety

Early mid-summer varieties (fruiting from June to early July):
 'Elvira', 'Honeoye', 'Rosie' (well, we've got to plant that one!)

Mid-summer varieties (fruiting through July):
 'Cambridge Favourite', 'Elsanta', 'Pegasus'

Late summer (mid-July to early August):
 'Alice', 'Florence', 'Maxim'

Perpetual varieties produce a modest amount of fruit throughout the summer, but the season can extend right into November:
 'Challenger', 'Mara des Bois', 'Vivarosa'

Tile mosaics

AGE RANGE	**Six years onwards**
TIME OF YEAR	**Early summer**

Paper and indelible marker

Gloves and safety goggles

Any tile, frost proof if to be used outside

Mosaic pieces on sheets or in bags

Old tiles (optional) to smash up and sort into pieces

Tile adhesive, waterproof if tiles are for outside

Spatula or old butter knife for spreading adhesive and grout

Grout, exterior grout if tiles are for outside

Sponge for wiping off excess grout (this needs to be damp)

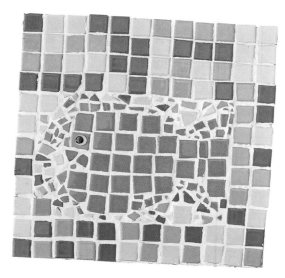

I still have a little shell mosaic I made at Brownie camp when I was ten years old. We all went to stay in Frinton and we collected shells from the beach and pressed them into a Polyfilla mix placed in a Dairy Lee triangle box! We pushed a hair grip into the mix at the top so it could be hung up when dry, and hung up it was, for years and years ... good old mum!

Tile mosaics are very straightforward to make; the key is in the preparation, and the beauty is that everyone can have a go. Ready-made mosaic tiles

are available in sheets to make everyone's life easier, or they can be bought loose in mixed bags. For our project we used a mixture of ready-made ones (see opposite) and pieces from old tiles that an adult carefully smashed inside a sturdy plastic bag (see overleaf). However, an older child could do this just as well under adult supervision. Whoever does the smashing must wear gloves and safety specs. For more detailed work, tile nippers can be used by adults to cut the tiles, but it is essential that goggles are worn to protect eyes.

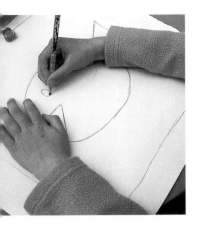
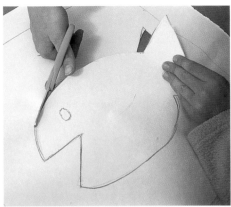
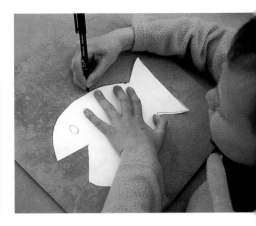

Draw the outline of your design onto paper.
Try to keep it as simple as possible for a stronger impact. Cut out the shape.

Place your design onto the tile that will be the base
of your mosaic and use an indelible marker to draw around the image.

If using old tiles, place
them in a sturdy plastic bag (like a rubble sack).

Carefully smash into small pieces with a hammer and
pour out the pieces onto an old tray. Remember to wear gloves and safety specs.

Sort the smashed tiles into shapes and colours. An assortment
of old plastic containers will be useful for this as any spares can be stored away for another day.

Apply tile adhesive to the area
of your design using a spatula or an old butter knife.

Gradually apply the mosaic tile pieces leaving small,
uniform gaps between them for the grout.

When all the pieces are in position, leave to dry (preferably for
24 hours) and then you can spread grout between the tiles. Do this either by hand or using a spatula.

Wipe off excess grout using a damp sponge
and then leave again for 24 hours before you install your tile in its chosen location.

Other decorative ideas

Tile cement can be spread thickly onto terracotta flower pots, with shells and beads pressed in to make perfect containers for succulents such as houseleeks (*Sempervivum*).

Spiral mound

AGE RANGE **Six years onwards**

TIME OF YEAR **Early summer**

Digger! (for something less ambitious, see below)

Whacker plate

Rubble or hardcore

Earth and top soil

Small sticks

String

Compost for the slopes and for planting the hornbeam

Hornbeam saplings (see the box on planting the spiral on page 67)

Bark chippings

Grass seed or a grass and wild flower seed mix

This is a project for those of you with plenty of space in your garden, as this spiral mound is 5m (5¼yd) in diameter at the base (of course, you could always make it smaller). Spirals are, in fact, labyrinths that go back thousands of years and are more popular now than ever. In our uncertain and often confusing times, people seem to find assurance in seeking a definite path. These are the days of far too many choices, so what a relief to have but one direction to go until you are finally King (or Queen) of the Castle!

We constructed our mound from the soil and spoil of another garden project and, certainly, if you have recently had an extension and are wondering what to do with a pile of rubble, this could be just the thing for swallowing it up! Our mate Ray came over and spent the day on a digger. First he created a solid base using hardcore and scalpings, which he compacted using a whacker plate, available from a tool hire shop. Then he built up the mound 30cm

(12in) at a time, compacting each layer of earth as he went. Thanks Ray! For a smaller mound, ask a builders' yard to deliver type 1 hardcore, which self-bonds when consolidated. It can be compacted by hand using a punner, which can also be hired.

Construct the mound (the adult part of the job – see opposite), making
sure there is room at the top for a circular den (ours was about 2m (2yd) in diameter at the top).

Mark out the spiral path (children can definitely help with this and
everything else there is to do for this splendid creation) with small sticks pushed into the ground and string tied between them. Then add a thin layer of compost to the sloping sides where the grass will be planted – this is optional, you might think your top soil doesn't need extra help.

Rake over the path to remove pebbles
and rocks and stamp it down to create a firm surface.

Following the **string marker** around the outside
edge of the spiral, dig a narrow trench to the depth of the saplings' previous planting.

Plant the hornbeam saplings in the
trench about 23cm (9in) apart all around the top of the mound, and then follow the path down using the stick and string markers for guidance.

Try to have as little direct contact with the roots as possible while arranging them. The trick is to have one person place the sapling carefully while another firms in the roots with compost. When all the tree saplings have been planted, give them a good watering.

Spread bark chippings over the path.

Sow grass seed (here we used a grass and wild flower mix) all over the compost-covered sides of the mound.

Water the mound regularly throughout the summer until the tree saplings and grass have established. You might find it easier to place a permanent water sprinkler at the top for the summer.

Planting the spiral

Hornbeam (*Carpinus*) is a slow-growing, hardy, native tree with green catkins from late spring to autumn, turning to clusters of winged fruit in the autumn, providing food for wildlife. Once the hedge has become established, the leaves turn brown but they will be retained through the winter – just like beech.

Some plants may not survive; check for healthy growth by making a tiny scratch at the base to see if there is any green beneath the bark.

Container-grown plants for hedging can be planted at any time of year, though preferably in spring or autumn. But bare-root plants are by far the cheapest way of making a hedge, and are available between autumn and early spring from forestry suppliers or your local garden centre or nursery.

Incorporate plenty of organic matter and bonemeal when planting to help the saplings establish quickly. They will need planting as soon as you get them home, or they can be temporarily planted in a trench to keep roots undamaged. Encourage more vigorous growth by cutting saplings up to half their height after planting; this will help to make them thicker. Thereafter, clip hornbeam hedges twice a year in early May and early September to keep them in shape.

Hopscotch path

AGE RANGE **Four years onwards**

TIME OF YEAR **Summer**

Bricks, slabs or pavers
Sharp sand
Cement
Screed board or spirit level
Mallet and board for levelling
Fine, kiln-dried sand

Making your choice

For our sunny, south-facing path we included the stunning blue flowers of *Veronica prostrata* as well as different thyme (*Thymus*) and chamomile (*Chamaemelum*) plants. These evergreen herbs creep between the bricks, releasing their scented aromas when jumped or hopped on, as well as producing pretty flowers. If your path is in a shadier position, you could use Corsican mint (*Mentha requienii*), which has a delicious peppermint scent, or the sweetly scented woodruff (*Galium odoratum*).

Hopscotch began during the early Roman Empire when Roman soldiers used the game for military training exercises. The children imitated them and the game has survived right into our 21st century! It is a great way for children to have exercise and fun at the same time as it involves throwing, hopping and trying not to fall over. It can be played alone or with friends simply by drawing the hopscotch squares onto the ground with chalk, and the game is suitable for anyone who can jump!

We have incorporated a set of hopscotch pavers into the path that leads to our shed. Making it is fairly straightforward, but it certainly needs an adult to oversee the project.

Dig out the area

where the path will be, allowing for the depth of the brick or slab, and the same depth again for the mortar mix. Our bricks were 6.5cm (2⅓in) deep, so we made our mortar mix 6.5cm (2⅓in) deep as well, making the total depth to dig out 13cm (about 5in).

Having cleared out the area of soil, sift through to remove any stones.

Fill the path area with the dry mortar mix, which should be roughly eight parts sharp sand to one part cement, mixed together well.

Level the mortar using a screed board or spirit level and then place the bricks or slabs on top. For our herringbone pattern we used eight bricks per 'square'.

For small paths, use a mallet and board to level the bricks (larger areas would require a whacker plate, available from a tool hire shop, but this must be used by an adult only).

Brush fine, kiln-dried sand between the bricks to lock them in place.

Apply a gritty soil around the edges
of the bricks or slabs.

Plant your herbs and small flowering plants
(see page 68) in the spaces between the hopscotch squares and
around the edges. They will soon creep over edges, softening
the overall look as well as suppressing weeds.

The rules of hopscotch

- The first player throws a pebble or some kind of marker onto the first square.

- They then hop over the square and hopscotch to the top without treading outside the squares, on any lines, or putting two feet down when they're supposed to be hopping.

- On returning to the square with the pebble on, they bend down and pick it up then hop or jump onto that square.

- Back at the start, the pebble is then thrown onto the next number, and so on until the last number has been reached.

- If you throw your pebble and miss the square then you miss your go, and the next player has their turn.

Chalk wall

Art is one of man's oldest and most basic means of expression, and the gateway to all creativity. Pablo Picasso once visited a children's art show and said, 'At that age I could draw like Raphael ... it took me years to learn to draw like these children.'

Encouraging children to draw and paint helps to give them a sense that they are important people who have ideas to share; moreover, creative play of all kinds is essential to a child's emotional and social development, helping to increase levels of independence, resourcefulness and confidence.

This outdoor blackboard will get the children outside as well as encouraging their artistic expression and, of course, it saves on paper! This is suitable for any child, as long as she or he can pick up some chalk and make marks. All you have to do is encourage and appreciate. We used slate, which is perfect for drawing on, but any smooth slab could be

used, such as York stone. Of course, ordinary paving slabs on the patio are suitable for drawing on if you don't have an appropriate wall on which to place the slate. To hang the slate on surfaces other than stone (see below), carefully drill through it – a good 3cm (1½ in) in from the edges – and screw it into a wood shed or other wall surface. Slate edges are sharp so they should be covered with wooden battens.

Cut into the wall with a hammer and chisel about 3cm (1¼ in) deep in the shape of the slate you are fixing. If you are going to be cutting into brick, you will need to hire an angle-grinder to mark out the area for the slate.

Fill with a strong mortar mix of three parts cement to one part soft sand and water.

Press the slate into the mix, smooth the edges with a trowel and leave to set overnight.

Sweet smells

Plant some lavender close by; the perfume will help to relax the children. Encourage them to rub it between their fingers to enjoy the wonderful aroma.

Making hypertufa pots

AGE RANGE **Eight years onwards**

TIME OF YEAR **Summer**

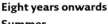

Two flowerpots, one at least two sizes larger than the other
Cooking oil
Kitchen roll
Peat substitute
Sieve
Bucket to mix the hypertufa in
Rubber gloves
Coarse sand or fine grit
Cement
Thin, plastic netting
Small sticks to place in drainage holes
Plastic bag
Decorating materials, e.g. children's non-toxic paints, shells, spare hypertufa mix, mosaic tiles, beads, twigs

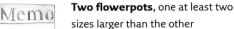

I have used hypertufa to cover old sinks to create a stone-like appearance, so for a small amount of cash I now have several stone-like containers at a fraction of the cost. Hypertufa is a mixture of peat substitute, coarse sand or fine grit, cement and water and needs about a week to dry. Pots are perfect for children to grow annual flowers or herbs in, or simply to collect snail shells and favourite stones.

Grease the inside of the larger flowerpot and the outside of the smaller pot with cooking oil.

Sieve some peat substitute into a bucket.

Add equal parts of coarse sand (or gravel, if using) and cement. Wearing rubber gloves, mix together.

Add sufficient water to make a thick paste, stirring all the time.

Apply the paste to the oiled inside of the larger pot, as if lining the sides.

Insert plastic netting into the hypertufa pot to help give the mixture strength. Then apply a further thin layer of the mix over the netting.

Insert the small pot to help the hypertufa maintain a pot shape. Level the top with a flat edge, like an old spoon.

Insert small sticks through the drainage holes so they touch the small pot and are protruding from the bottom of the larger pot.

Cover the whole thing with a plastic bag and leave to dry for about a week.

Once fully dry, remove the bag, sticks and inner pot. Then cut off the outer pot – definitely a job for an adult.

Take care when removing the pot as cut plastic edges are sharp.

Snip off any visible pieces of netting.

Use the sticks to ensure the drainage holes are clear by pushing them through a few times.

Now decorate your pot
– for ideas for decorating hypertufa and other surfaces, see overleaf.

Decorating pots

Decorating your homemade pots means that you can add whatever finishing touches you like. Paint your hypertufa pot in bright colours using children's paint, maybe incorporating stamps and stencils, or glue shells to the surface. Alternatively, if you have some hypertufa left over you can use it to decorate existing pots. Here's how ...

Score the surface of the pot and

apply the hypertufa to the surface in your chosen shape (we made a snake). To aid adhesion further, use PVA glue and allow it to become tacky.

Leave to dry

for several days before painting.

If your decorated pot is going to be left outside, apply several coats of exterior varnish (always allowing it to dry between coats) to ensure it is waterproof.

Mosaic tiles

When hypertufa is not to hand, decorating a pot for your favourite plant can still be great fun. There are many different children's kits available to choose from or you can buy your own materials.

Miniature mosaic tiles are easy to stick on with rubber-based glue and you can create any number of different patterns. These are not waterproof, so use pots decorated in this way indoors only.

Car track

AGE RANGE **Six years onwards**

TIME OF YEAR **Summer**

Stick, sand or spray paint

Cement

Sharp sand

Metal float for levelling

Turf

Water-based external paint

Paintbrush

Chalk

It's curious how, when it comes to cars, boys – both big and small – just can't resist getting in on the action. Hal and Harry really enjoyed making a racing track to play cars outside, and even Rose had a go. We made our track in a spare part of the vegetable garden where we have raised beds.

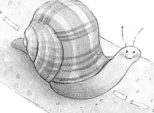

Mark out the shape of your track onto the soil (we used sticks, but you could use sand or spray paint). Our track is a figure of eight, which keeps the whole track within a child's reach.

Dig out a trench for the track, roughly 10cm (4in) deep and 15cm (6in) wide.

Mix together six parts of cement to one part of sharp sand and pour in enough water to make the mixture pliable. Stir thoroughly.

Gradually **fill the trench** with cement and use a metal float to level off the track, creating a flat surface. Leave to dry for 12 hours.

Lay turf around the track.

Paint the track and once more leave to dry. Use chalk to draw road markings, or paint for more permanent patterns.

WATER

Children will always enjoy water, whether it is splashing about in a paddling pool or floating small boats in a shallow, plastic tray. Running through water on a hot day is a great favourite for cooling down, while splashing in puddles with welly boots never fails to please. Harry and Rose have often spent ages together washing up their plastic plates and cups in a tub placed on the patio filled with warm, soapy water. Collect a selection of different plastic containers for children to fill up with water and perhaps put holes in the base of some to create a shower. Simple play things like this are often far more popular than expensive toys.

Have fun with frozen water too by making frozen flower ice cubes. Simply pour drinking water into an ice-cube tray only half way up, and place small flowers or petals into each cube. Put in the freezer until solid, remove and add more water to bring the level up to the top of the tray, and then freeze. Use a selection of edible flowers such as borage (*Borago officinalis*), pot marigolds (*Calendula officinalis*), cowslips (*Primula veris*), nasturtium (*Tropaeolum majus*) and roses (*Rosa*).

However, because children will always be drawn to water ensure you provide safe water experiences. It could be said that the only childproof kind of water feature is one where there is no standing water, such as a bubble fountain where a water reservoir is hidden under the ground and water pumped up through a drilled hole (such as this replica ammonite).

Wall-mounted water features, such as our 'Arthur' here, are also a safe option, but only if the container that holds the water on the ground is covered with a grate (we also planted some water loving plants like this *Equisetum hyemale*.)

A wildlife pond is fairly child friendly, but I would say not at all toddler friendly. However, a pond in a container, such as the one we made with Rose (see overleaf), is a good compromise where safety is of concern for older children. But, again, it is only safe if young toddlers aren't around. Instead, for the best fun in the garden, you can do no better than a hose, which can be attached to a number of different playthings, including the garden shower, crazy daisy or the ever popular water slide.

Of course, a hard fall in a bad position on slippery surfaces can result in injury, so it is important to monitor all activity in the garden where water is concerned ... and always have a large pile of towels to hand!

Rose's aquatic garden

AGE RANGE **Four years onwards**
TIME OF YEAR **Summer**

Large, watertight container
Bricks and other stones
Water, preferably rainwater
Plants, see page 84

Where children are concerned, water in the garden can be a real worry, especially as it only takes a few centimetres of water to pose a real threat of drowning. Even this water garden in a container is not entirely child-friendly if there are toddlers about, so site it where you can keep an eye on it. Our sunny, sheltered patio is the perfect place for our water garden, but in the winter you will need to put your water garden under cover so it doesn't freeze, or alternatively drain it and store the plants in a frost-free environment.

Almost any container, from plastic bins to glazed pots, can be used, as long as it is watertight. Galvanised containers are safe to use for tadpoles or fish if you first paint the container with black bitumastic paint to seal in the zinc. Check you have fish friendly paint by buying it at a specialist water garden centre.

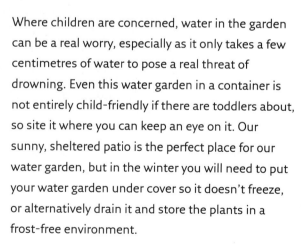

Position the container in its final location
where there is plenty of sunshine and partial shade, checking that it is level.
We used an old galvanised tub.

Stack up some bricks in the tub
on which to place some of the marginal plants; some prefer a
water depth of only 2.5–5cm (1–2in).

Provide a step
(or ramp) for wildlife to be able to get in
and out. We used a cobblestone brick.

Fill the container **with rainwater,** if possible, or allow tap
water to stand for at least 48 hours to allow chlorine and other chemicals to
dissipate before planting anything or adding wildlife. Tap water has chemicals
in it that can kill tadpoles.

Position any final stones
and start filling your pond – see overleaf.

Consider buying a ready-planted basket of marginal plants from a local aquatic centre

(see below) and carefully place it in the water. If buying separate plants, always check the depth at which each one prefers to be planted. In hot weather, ensure your garden remains topped up with water.

For tadpoles, seek out a friend with a pond and

catch some in a jar. Ensure your container has been painted with black bitumastic paint (see page 82) and then carefully pour the tadpoles into the aquatic garden. Tadpoles love a pinch of lettuce a day!

Surround your water garden with a selection of container grown plants

to complete the picture or plant up some containers with cheap and colourful bedding plants.

What plants?

You can buy ready-planted baskets in various sizes. One for a container our size could include a small water lily (e.g. *Nymphaea pygmaea* 'Alba'); two marginal plants, e.g. marsh marigold and bog bean (*Caltha palustris* and *Menyanthes trifoliate*); a floater, e.g. water hyacinth (*Eichhornia crassipes*); and a submerged plant, e.g. Canadian pondweed (*Elodea canadensis*).

Harry's bog garden

AGE RANGE **Six years onwards**
TIME OF YEAR **Summer**
YOU WILL NEED **Wheelbarrow** (we used a plastic one)
or other plastic or galvanised container
Hammer and nail
Large crocks
Shingle
Multipurpose compost
Rich organic matter, we used
well rotted garden compost
Moisture loving plants, enough for
dense planting (see page 87)
Bark chippings or gravel

Harry made a container bog garden to sit on the patio; he really enjoyed mucking about with the soil. Often people make bog gardens and ponds adjacent to each other where the water can run from one into the other. This can cause major problems for the pond as soil will bring nutrients into the pond water, which can turn the water green or choke it with blanket weed. By planting in a container you can avoid those problems, and you don't even need to have a garden.

We've made our bog garden in an old plastic wheelbarrow, placing it in a sheltered sunny spot with partial shade, which is essential for any bog garden. In a cold winter, the wheelbarrow can easily be wheeled into the shed or garage until the growth starts again the following spring.

Bog gardens need slow drainage but also sufficient moisture retention for the moisture loving plants – the soil must never be allowed to dry out. You could use any watertight container, just so long as you can provide adequate drainage and a depth of at least 30cm (12in) of compost. Occasionally apply a weak, balanced liquid fertiliser to encourage lush growth in the growing season.

Punch drainage holes into the base of your container (about five holes per 10cm sq) using a nail and hammer – this is strictly an adult job.

Line the bottom with large crocks over the holes, plus a layer of shingle to prevent the holes from clogging up. The drainage assisted by the crocks and shingle prevent stagnation.

Shovel in a mixture of multipurpose compost and rich organic matter, which will greatly improve water retentiveness. Aquatic composts are available, and usually contain slow-release fertilisers in their mix.

Put on some gloves and mix it together.
Water thoroughly; the plants will need lots of moisture.

Roughly **position your plants** while still in their containers, thinking about the contrast of foliage shapes and textures.

Dig holes for each plant and firm them in gently. Mulch with chipped bark or gravel to help retain moisture and prevent weeds.

Irrigate with rainwater rather than tap water, never letting the bog garden dry out.

Choosing your plants

Plants we used were:

Blue satin flower (*Sisyrinchium angustifolium*), forget-me-not (*Myosotis palustris* 'Semperflorens'), horsetail rush (*Equisetum fluviatile*), *Hosta*, *Ligularia przewalskii*, sweet flat (*Acorus gramineus* 'Ogon') and water dropwort (*Oenanthe fistulosa* 'Flamingo').

Other moisture loving plants include:

Astilbe, *Brunnera macrophylla*, Candleabra primula (*Primula japonica*), dagger leaf rush (*Juncus ensifolius*), European globeflower (*Trollius europaeus*), gardener's garters (*Phalaris arundinacea* var *picta*) and *Lobelia cardinalis*.

Giant moisture loving plants will need a much larger container, such as an old trough or bath, but would be great fun to grow towering above the children, filling them with awe. These plants include Chinese rhubarb (*Rheum palmatum* 'Atrosanguineum'), the huge leaved *Gunnera manicata*, and the Royal fern (*Osmunda regalis*).

Sensory garden

AGE RANGE **Two years onwards** to rub leaves

TIME OF YEAR **Summer**

One or two tyres per planter
(we chose fairly large tyres)

Old plastic flowerpots

Organic matter - lots

Multipurpose compost

Water-retaining granules

Sense enhancing flowers (see my
suggestions for plants that will tantilise
each sense on pages 91–5)

Mulch

All gardens are sensory to some degree, but I thought it would be fun to create a specific area for children to come into direct contact with their five senses, where they can explore plants safely without the worry that they may be touching a potentially harmful plant. I decided to use old tyres as planters and we painted them bright colours. Tyres are also good for smaller children to sit on, they're cheap (or free) and, of course, it's good to recycle them. Raising the height of plants in this way provides easy access for the children, and is especially helpful to the vision-impaired or wheelchair user. I also planted several different coloured buddleias (*Buddleja*) around the perimeter of the garden to attract butterflies. To improve flowering, prune the buddleia back hard to a low framework each spring.

For added sensory interest we also built this set of huge wooden 'chime bars'. Using woods of different densities means each stick sounds at a different pitch when hit. Music to the ears!

Position each tyre (or tyres – we used two, one on top of the other, for depth and height) on level ground.

Line the bottom of the tyres with upside down plastic flowerpots to help fill the volume – the tyres are quite large and deep. This also assists with drainage.

Throw in lots of organic matter, such as garden compost, to help retain moisture and supply the container with humus and nutrients.

Mix in some multipurpose compost to the top of the tyres together with water-retaining granules. These granules are great for helping containers to retain their moisture, particularly through the warm months, although you'll still need to water the containers regularly.

Before starting to **plant,** water the compost thoroughly.

Choose the plants for each tyre – the fun bit – and plant up, firming them well into place.
We planted one set of tyres for each sense – see pages 91–5. Water the tyres thoroughly again.

Add a mulch to retain moisture and inhibit weeds. This could include gravel, cocoa shells or small bark chippings.

For extra colour, you could plant seeds of annuals
by gently pushing them into the compost (see page 126). I used an annual wildflower mix of corn poppy (*Papaver rhoeas*), corn marigold (*Chrysanthemum segetum*), cornflower (*Centaurea cyanus*) and corn cockle (*Agrostemma*).

Smell

Whether a plant smells good or not really depends on personal taste, and the plant world has us spoilt for choice. Some plants need to be touched to activate their scent, such as honey bush (*Melianthus major*), whose foliage quite unexpectedly smells of peanuts when rubbed. Others, like the deliciously scented rose, pump out their fragrance. Delight your children with pineapple, chocolate and bubble gum smells, while promoting an awareness and respect for their natural environment at the same time.

Melianthus major

Plants with fruity or sweet smells include:

Agastache foeniculum (anise hyssop). A hardy perennial with a distinctive aniseed-like scent, smelling just like liquorice, which is made from aniseed.

Azara microphylla. This evergreen shrub does best against a sheltered, sunny wall. It has small banana-scented flowers in late winter/early spring.

Cercidiphyllum japonicum (katsura tree). This deciduous tree has fantastic autumn foliage that smells of toffee.

Chamaemelum nobile 'Treneague'. A non-flowering chamomile whose foliage smells deliciously fruity when gently crushed.

Cosmos atrosanguineus (chocolate cosmos). Now here's a

plant that really does smell of chocolate, guaranteed to astonish adults as much as children. This plant is not completely hardy, but should survive most winters if you cover it with a good thick layer of mulch.

Mentha x *piperita* (chocolate mint). This mint has the distinctive aroma of those after-dinner mint chocolates 'After Eight' – in fact, there is a variety called just that! Simply crush the leaves between your fingers and take a deep breath ... what a fantastic smell!

Cytisus battandieri (pineapple broom). A semi-evergreen shrub that does best by a sheltered, sunny wall. Bright yellow pineapple-scented flowers even look a bit pineapple-like!

Helichrysum angustifolium (curry plant). As the common name suggests, this plant has a very strong curry scent, which pleases my children as they are particularly fond of Indian food!

Jasminum officinale (jasmine). A strong, semi-deciduous climber with small white summer flowers that are intensely sweet.

Melianthus major (honey bush). I chose this plant for our sensory garden for two reasons. One is the fabulous foliage, which is jagged and blue-green in colour, and can reach over 2m (6½ft) high. The other is the unmistakeable whiff of peanuts when you rub the foliage – a must for all peanut butter fans.

Mentha suaveolens (apple mint). This mint has fresh, fruity, aromatic leaves as well as fragrant flowers, and attracts bees and butterflies. All mints should be confined to some kind of container because of their invasive nature.

Pelargonium. Scented-leaved pelargoniums have extremely aromatic foliage in a wide range of perfumes, including lemon, chocolate, strawberry, peach and ginger. These tender plants need to be kept in frost-free conditions over winter, and re-potted each spring.

Trachelospermum jasminoides (star jasmine). Evergreen climber with creamy-white flowers during mid- to late summer, which smell delicious.

Viola odorata (sweet violets). These lovely little plants thrive in rich soil and shady corners. They are known as sweet violets because of their sweet-tasting flower (who remembers those lovely violet sweets?). Will self-seed happily or can be grown in containers for little noses to sniff more easily.

Sight

The sight of a giant cardoon (*Cynara cardunculus*) would fill anyone with wonder, but imagine the impact of this towering perennial on a small child. I remember vividly the stunning delphiniums my best friend's mum used to grow – I never realised plants could have such intense colour, and I was amazed. Learning to really look at things such as colour, shape, pattern or texture can only stimulate and enhance our enjoyment of whatever we see. These are the things I learned at art college a long time ago, but now I'm not painting with oils anymore, I'm painting with plants instead! Experimenting with colour can take a lifetime to master, but don't be put off trying out different colour combinations. More often than not, nature will just take over anyway, and suddenly a self-seeded plant will turn up and upstage your meticulously made grand plans!

Giant plants to inspire awe include:

Allium giganteum. Excellent bulb for majesterial height.

Angelica archangelica (angelica). This eye-catching biennial can reach 2m (over 6ft) with domed flower heads and magnificent foliage.

Crambe cordifolia. The stems of this perennial can reach a dramatic 2.5m (8ft) and are crowded with tiny, honey-scented flowers in early summer.

Cynara cardunculus (cardoon). This silver-leaved plant has large, thistle-like flowers and can reach 1.5m (5ft) high.

Ferula communis (giant fennel). A hardy herbaceous perennial with a massive mound of feathery leaves and yellow flowers in early summer that reaches a mighty 3m (10ft) in height!

Gunnera manicata (giant rhubarb). A massive moisture-loving plant that can tower over small children.

Nectaroscordum siculum subsp. *bulgaricum*. This bulb has succulent 1.2m (4ft) stems and bell-shaped flowers that look like miniature fairy castles when they up-turn into their seed head state.

Onopordum acanthium (Scotch thistle). This silver-leaved plant can reach the mighty height of 2.5m (8ft).

Rheum palmatum 'Atrosanguineum' (ornamental rhubarb). A moisture-loving plant with massive foliage, able to reach a height of 2.5m (8ft).

Rudbeckia 'Herbstonne'. The golden daisy-like flowers emerge at the top of giant 2.2m (7ft) stems.

Sound

As a child I loved the sound of the rain on my tent while I snuggled up warm in my sleeping bag. I still love the noise, and open all the doors and windows on rainy summer days. The calming sound of summer rain can be captured on rainless days by a gentle, bubbling water feature, perfect for soothing the senses. We placed a simple birdbath in our sensory garden, which is safe and easy to keep topped up with a watering can (toddlers must always be supervised around water; even just a few centimetres can be dangerous). On quiet mornings (that's *before* the children wake up!), I love to wander around the garden listening to the wind's movement through the trees, the gentle hum of bees and the sweet songs of birds.

In our sensory garden, I've placed wind chimes to help create a relaxing atmosphere for the children as they wander from one tyre container to the next, rubbing, tasting and smelling the plants. Of course, children aren't always in a mood to relax, so noisier moods are catered for by the wooden xylophone made from thick sticks of elder, sycamore, holly, buddleia, hornbeam, aspen, willow, birch and lime. It is remarkable just how musical wood is in such a raw state, and children love comparing the different tones of each stick (so do adults!).

Musical plants include:

Briza media (**quaking grass**). A very pretty perennial grass *(below right)* that rattles in the breeze.

Cortaderia selloana (**pampas grass**). This rustles softly in a breeze.

Lunaria annua (**honesty**). This spring flowering plant *(middle right)* has disc-like translucent seed heads that have earned it its other common name, money plant.

Miscanthus sinensis '**Silberfeder**'. Miscanthus are elegant, late-flowering grasses above mounds of arching leaves.

Papaver somniferum (**opium poppy**). The large seed heads on this plant rattle. Don't be scared of the common name – poppy seeds from this flower are edible!

Phylostachys vivax '**Aureocaulis**'. Bamboos make good screening and will help to disguise nearby traffic noise as their stems and leaves whisper in the wind.

Populus tremula '**Pendula**' (**weeping aspen**). This weeping tree is suited to an average-sized garden; other poplars grow tall and fast and should never be planted near buildings. Flat leaf stems make a fluttering sound in the wind.

Stipa gigantea (**feather grass**). Tall, elegant grass plumes catch the breeze. This is one of my favourite grasses.

Taste

Growing your own fruit and vegetables is not as complicated as it is often made out to be. If you don't have a garden or much space, simply grow your produce in containers, keep them watered and before you know it, you'll be nibbling on delicious home grown treats of sweet fresh peas, strawberries or juicy tomatoes.

Of course, it is essential to ensure children remain cautious about eating things from the garden, as poisonous berries can easily be mistaken for sweet treats. Spend time in the garden with your children, showing them around the plants that are safe and those to be avoided. I planted wild strawberries, which produce sweet, miniature fruit as well as tumbling tomatoes (even notorious plant-killers can grow these successfully!) – see pages 58 and 52.

Some unusual vegetables for you to try

Cucumbers. 'Crystal Lemon' cucumbers, also known as 'Crystal Apple' grow successfully outside and produce delicious, pale round fruit that look just like lemons. Can be grown up a tripod or on the ground.

Kidney bean 'Black and White'. A dwarf French bean whose distinctive black and white markings resemble Orca the Killer Whale. Produce succulent green 'French bean' pods, and highly ornamental black and white 'Haricot' beans for use in soup and stews.

Sweetcorn 'Strawberry Popcorn'. This sweetcorn looks like oval-shaped, pink golf balls. Sweetcorn is easy to grow, tasting great raw, or dried cobs can be put into the microwave to make popcorn! Plant in blocks rather than in rows to ensure good pollination and grow in a sunny, sheltered position.

Tomatillo. These look like green tomatoes, but are enclosed in a silk-like skin and taste sweet and tangy, especially if they're ripe and turning yellow.

Vegetable spaghetti (*Cucurbito pepo*). This is a member of the winter squash family, which includes pumpkins and butternut squash and can be grown just like a pumpkin. Inside the butter coloured exterior is long, thin spaghetti-like flesh that can be served with sauce just like pasta!

Potatoes. These can be grown successfully in a container at least 30cm (12in) deep and wide. Crock the base for drainage, and then add 10cm (4in) of a loam-based compost. Plant three tubers per pot and cover with 15cm (6in) of compost and, as the foliage grows, earth up the potatoes until the container is full. Seed potatoes are available from garden centres from February. Home bought potatoes can be used, too, but are usually treated to retard sprouting, and even if they do sprout they won't produce as well ... but perhaps they are worth a try in a container. (Bear in mind that leaves of the potato plant are poisonous.)

Touch

From the satin sheen coat of a beautifully bred racehorse (*Prunus serrula*) to cuddly, fluffy lambs' ears (*Stachys byzantina*), plants conjure many images purely through touch. Touch is possibly the least explored of our senses in the garden, as many of us are content to stand and stare, but once the gloves are off, the plants can pack their final punch – some painfully, such as the viciously pointed tips of *Agave americana* or *Yucca filamentosa* (definitely not a plant to have if children are about). Children can be taught how plants adapt their foliage to protect themselves from the elements as well as from pests. For instance, the fine fur on many silver-leaved plants such as *Stachys* helps to protect the leaves from the sun by deflecting light and trapping moisture, while spines stop them from being eaten by hungry herbivores.

Stachys byzantina

Touchy feely plants include:

Allium hollandicum 'Purple Sensation'. The perfect, purple globes on these ornamental onions look solid enough but feel so delicate to the touch.

Ballota pseudodictamnus. Grey-white leaves feel like felt. A lovely foliage plant for dry conditions.

Bassia scoparia f. *trichophylla* (burning bush). This is a half-hardy annual of finely divided foliage just asking to be stroked or hugged.

Foeniculum vulgare (fennel). Feathery, aromatic leaves.

Helianthus 'Teddy Bear'. Baby sunflowers with soft, fluffy pompon heads.

Lagurus ovatus (hare's tail). It's irresistible to touch the furry, oval flower heads on this easily grown hardy annual.

Lavandula stoechas subsp. *pedunculata* (papillon or butterfly lavender). This aromatic evergreen has rose-purple bracts on top of the flowers, which look like bunnies' ears or butterflies.

Lychnis coronaria (rose campion). This biennial plant will self-seed profusely, which is no bad thing, as its soft, downy leaves are lovely to touch. It has an added bonus of beautiful bright magenta flowers.

Papaver orientale (Oriental poppy). Hairy foliage contrasts with the satin sheen of the tissue paper-like petals.

Pennisetum alopecuroides (fountain grass). The grass heads feel like fat hairy caterpillars.

Potentilla atrosanguinea. A summer flowering perennial with the softest, silvery haired leaves.

Pulsatilla vulgaris (pasqueflower). In addition to silk-wrapped buds, pasqueflowers have purple flowers, which turn into beautiful silky seed heads.

Salix caprea 'Kilmarnock'. A small, weeping tree with silvery catkins in spring.

Salvia argentea (sage). Perennial with woolly, silver leaves.

Stachys byzantina (lamb's ears). This evergreen perennial is completely hardy, and one of the first plants in spring to develop a thick carpet of woolly leaves. The floppy leaves are extremely reminiscent of baby lambs' ears, both to feel and to look at. It is a cuddly plant children will want to stroke.

Stipa tenuissima 'Ponytails'. This is a lovely ornamental grass for children to run their fingers through. The soft, grassy plumes look just like wispy pony tails.

Verbascum bombyciferum (giant silver mullein). These white, woolly, yellow-flowered spires look snow covered, though they become quite prickly later in the summer.

Naturalising bulbs

AGE RANGE **Six years onwards**

TIME OF YEAR **Summer–autumn**

Bulbs suitable for naturalising
(see opposite)

Compost

I have a very strong memory of finding a bulb in our garden when I was seven years old, planting it in a little red bucket and taking it to Brownies. Brown Owl must have been sufficiently impressed as she awarded me a nature badge, although I don't ever remember seeing it flower. I expect the bulb rotted as my seaside bucket had no drainage holes in it, but it was the thought that counted!

Naturalising bulbs means that they are left to grow either in grassland or woodland where they will increase without interference, so once you've planted a group you can sit back and enjoy them spreading year after year. Obviously, a rough grass area is better than your lovingly tended lawn, as leaves from bulbs need to be left for six weeks after flowering. During this time, leaves produce food for the developing bulbs below the ground, which ensures a good display for the following year.

With autumn flowering bulbs, grass should not be cut after the beginning of September as the shoots need to be left to develop. Choose a semi-wild area at the back of the lawn, or a circle of uncut grass under a deciduous tree, or, if lawn maintenance is an issue, plant early flowering bulbs such as those listed in the winter section opposite.

Darcey and I planted *Colchicum autumnale* and *Crocus speciosus* in late summer (earlier than planting for spring bulbs, which is in autumn). Colchicum are large bulbs the size of a small apple and are poisonous, so are not suitable for children to plant (I planted those ones). Darcey planted *Crocus speciosus*.

Take handfuls of bulbs and gently throw them across the grass.

Plant the bulbs. To achieve a natural effect, do this where they land. Carefully lift the turf and dig a hole so each bulb is covered with roughly three times the depth of soil as the size of the bulb. We used a garden trowel to do this.

Pop in the bulb and cover with fresh compost and soil.

Re-position the cut turf, firming down gently. Water thoroughly.

After bulbs have **finished flowering,** leave the foliage for six weeks before clearing away.

Planting choices

When planting in containers, use a soil-based compost such as John Innes No. 3, and add one part grit for good drainage. Bulbs hate cold, waterlogged soil so drainage is essential, and avoid multipurpose compost, which can get very soggy and rot bulbs in winter.

Always make sure the base of any container has crocks put over the drainage holes, and place the containers in a sunny, sheltered spot. Heavy and prolonged frost can freeze containers so, wherever possible, move your pots close to the house, or under cover to prevent frost damage.

Bulbs suitable for naturalising include:

Winter: *Anemone blanda, Crocus tommasinianus, Cyclamen coum, Narcissus* 'February Gold', snowdrop (*Galanthus nivalis*) and winter aconite (*Eranthis hyemalis*).

Spring: bluebells (*Hyacinthoides non-scripta*), grape hyacinth (*Muscari armeniacum*) and Lent lily (*Narcissus pseudonarcissus*).

Summer: *Gladiolus byzantinus* and quamash (*Camassia leichtlinii*).

Autumn: autumn crocus (*Crocus speciosus*), *Cyclamen hederifolium* and naked ladies (*Colchicum autumnale*).

Action Man jungle

AGE RANGE **Four years onwards**

TIME OF YEAR **Summer–autumn**

Old telegraph pole
Spade
Concrete
Sharp sand
Screws and screwdriver
Bark chipping

We are all too aware of the soaring rate of obesity in children throughout developed countries. Much of the blame has been directed at poor diet and an excess of fatty foods, which has clearly played a part. However, the single most important factor is lack of exercise (and that goes for all of us!).

Many gardens have old, overgrown shrubberies that are perfect for this project, providing an instant 'jungle effect'. We used an old telegraph pole for stepping stone logs as well as a balancing pole, and created a tunnel to add a sense of adventure and mystery. Our tunnel is made from willow rods left over from the Willow den (see page 42). They create a natural-looking tunnel that blends in perfectly with the surrounding shrubs. Follow the planting instructions on page 43 and then bend and tie to shape. Alternatively, use bamboo canes to create a wigwam-type tunnel, or simply make a clearing through some established shrubs.

Our swing hangs close by from an old willow tree, but a climbing rope could be used, or an old tyre on a rope. The idea is to supply enough different possibilities for creating an action-packed area that's full of fun while helping to keep our kids fit. But keep them safe too – lay down a 25cm (10in) layer of bark chippings beneath your jungle.

While this is a project for an adult to make, involve your children in the decision making.

Create circular stepping logs by cutting them from an old telegraph pole

(we used a licensed chainsaw person).

Dig holes of various depths and slightly wider than the pole diameter.
The holes should be no shallower than 30cm (1ft) deep.

Place the **cut logs** in the holes (we arranged them
so that each log step was slightly higher than the previous one,
creating a stair-like arrangement).

Use a **strong dry mix** of eight parts concrete to one part
sharp sand, and push in firmly around the logs in the hole. Leave to set overnight.

For the **balancing pole,** use the rest of the telegraph pole.
Place a support post at either end of the balancing pole, fixing both of them in the
ground as for the stepping logs (see above).

Cut half way through the balancing pole at each end
so it sits level on the supporting posts.

Screw through from the top at each
end to secure. (We used three screws at each end; you might
want to use more.

Put down a deep layer of **bark chippings.**

NATURE

My first memories of nature are of my brother and me **mucking about** in our garden as toddlers. I remember the old apple tree at the bottom of the garden, the raspberries that our neighbour grew pushing through our fence, and the smell of roses we collected to make bottles of rose water. Ask anyone of their

earliest memories and among them will always be an **encounter** with nature, whether it be the smell of the earth, the touch of a prickly blackberry bush, the first sight of a rainbow, collecting tadpoles in a glass jar, or the sound of rain on a tent. Children have an affinity with nature, and I believe a basic need to **feel connected** somehow to the planet on which they live. By helping our children to engage with the natural world around them, we instil wonder, respect and compassion for a natural world that is increasingly under threat.

Nothing is more delightful in a garden than the sight of **playful butterflies** dancing in the breeze, or the beauty of their jewelled wings quivering on plants and sunbathing on paving. Buddleia is one of the major nectar-rich flowering plants that butterflies love but don't forget that butterflies were once **caterpillars,** and they also need to be considered. A patch of nettles, thistles, holly, grasses or bramble in full sun is ideal for them.

Attract the birds and the bees, too, by providing food, water and shelter, and they will reward you by bringing your garden to life. Ornamental and wild grasses, fruits, berries and thistle-like plants all provide food, while plants that produce seed heads in autumn, such as teasel (*Dipsacus fullonum*), are a tasty pre-winter snack. Trees, shrubs and climbers provide shelter and places

to make nests. The sweet songs and chatter of birds along with the gentle hum of a busy bee are things easily taken for granted, but with the numbers of many species of wildlife falling due to the disappearance of natural habitats such as hedgerows, meadows and woodlands, it is essential we all take some responsibility to redress the balance. Tempting birds into your garden will also help gardeners deal with pest control, as they feast on slugs, snails and other garden pests. Let's hear it for the birds!

Flowers depend on insects for pollination and seed production, but insects are also important for keeping pests under control, such as ladybirds, who have a large appetite for aphids, or ground beetles, which love munching on slugs. Worms (see page 112) are great composters, and insects of all kinds provide food for birds and other wildlife.

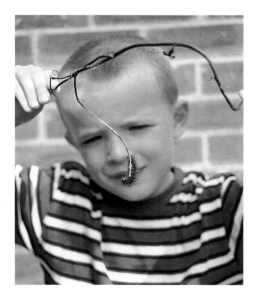

Butterfly farm

AGE RANGE **Six years onwards**

TIME OF YEAR **Summer–autumn**

Butterfly kit (mail order)

Wooden dowelling

Wood glue

Old fish tank with lid

Piece of linen and stapler

A butterfly darting haphazardly around the garden is wonderfully evocative of lazy summer afternoons, with the children tiptoeing to get close enough to study the elaborate markings before it flutters off to the next flower in search of nectar.

Children study life cycles at school so this practical introduction is certainly educational, but is also hugely rewarding. We sent off for our Red Admiral butterflies from an internet mail order service. Once you have paid, you receive an order card that, at the appropriate time, you complete and return. The exciting package arrives seven to ten days later by post.

The caterpillars arrive in a plastic container, which is their home for the first stage of their life cycle. There are ventilation holes and an adequate supply of food. Keep the container upright at a steady temperature (22–24°C) and away from direct sunlight for one to two weeks – the caterpillars increase in size quite dramatically. When they are ready to become chrysalides, they climb to the top of the container and attach themselves by their tails to the paper disc inside the lid and hang down in the shape of a letter 'J'. Now it is time to prepare their hatching habitat.

Make a frame from wooden dowelling stuck together with wood glue to sit snugly inside the back of the fish tank. Stretch a piece of linen taut across the frame and staple it securely. Then put the screen inside the tank.

Once all the **caterpillars** have turned into chrysalides, remove the lid of the container and take out the paper disc from which they are hanging. Do this very carefully. If the chrysalides sense danger, they will vibrate furiously – this is nothing to be concerned about, it's their way of deterring predators.

Pin the disc vertically to the linen with the chrysalides hanging flush against the disc.

After about ten days you may be able to detect the butterfly's colouring through the chrysalis shell.

see page 127.

Attracting butterflies to your garden

By combining nectar-producing plants and food plants for the caterpillars, butterflies can be encouraged to breed in your garden. Selecting plants with a combined flowering season – for example, wallflowers (*Erysimum*) and primroses (*Primula*) for spring and then lavender (*Lavandula*) and buddleia (*Buddleja*) for summer, with *Verbena* and Michaelmas daisy (*Aster movi-belgii*) for autumn – provides season-long nourishment. Place a couple of large, flat stones among the flowers for basking, too. For other plants that attract butterflies, see page 127.

A small area of wild, untidy garden provides a perfect habitat. Why not create a small area of 'meadow' with wildflowers grown from seeds?

Within a day or so, a series of **splits** will appear along the length of each chrysalis from which the butterfly's body will emerge.

You will probably notice a **red liquid** staining the disc or the linen. Although it resembles blood – and it can concern children – it is a residue of dye, unused from colouring the wings.

Furnish the tank with **fresh flowers** and leaves, and feed the butterflies with drops of 2 tsp sugar mixed with 200ml (7fl oz) fresh water. Use a pipette provided with the caterpillar kit and drop the food onto the leaves and petals, and some cotton make-up pads.

Feed the butterflies twice a day for two days – and then it's time to set them free.

Miniature farm

AGE RANGE **Six years onwards**

TIME OF YEAR **Summer–autumn**

Large shallow plastic tray with drainage holes

Multipurpose compost

Two pieces of turf

Sticks

Willow branches for weaving; we used young and malleable branches from our willow tree with the leaves stripped off but if no willow is available you could use any supple new growth from shrubs or climbers

Garden twine

Small plastic dish

Gravel

Straw

Plants, we used a baby box (*Buxus sempervirens* 'Suffruticosa') and dried seed heads of the opium poppy (*Papaver somniferum*)

Old plastic flowerpot

I first discovered the delights of making miniature gardens when I was eight years old. The primary school I attended held yearly Easter competitions, and I've been delighted to discover that the school our two children attend does the same thing. Last year, a few mums and I got together at our house and with the children we made miniature gardens in seed trays – only using what we could find here in our garden.

It was fascinating to see the different approaches all the children took to their own garden fantasy, and lovely to see the adults working with them to achieve their goal. With a little imagination, your perfect garden can be achieved without spending a penny. Now that's what I call a garden makeover! For this project, we've developed the garden one step further by making a miniature farm, although the ideas can be easily adapted for a miniature garden instead.

Put a layer of multipurpose compost on the bottom of the tray, leaving enough room on top to place the turf.

Water the compost thoroughly – this will help to compact the soil and to keep the turf moist.

Lay the turf. We used two pieces of turf, one for the meadow and one for underneath the barn (of course, you could always just use sawdust or straw for the barn floor). An adult should cut the turf to size – this can be harder than it looks. A long sharp knife will help with the shaping.

Water thoroughly, and press down hard on the turfs to firm them in place.

Cut several sticks (here we used willow) to about the same length – 18cm (6in). Insert them upright into the turf about 5cm (2in) apart, ready for weaving the barn walls.

Use willow branches to weave a fence. This can be a bit tricky as the branches need to be threaded in and out of the upright sticks, and small hands may need help.

Using garden twine, attach thicker **willow sticks** along the top of the frame to give the structure strength.

Weave two other willow fences for each side of the meadow in the same way.

To make a pond, use the small plastic dish. Fill the area between the barn and the meadow with gravel and add straw to the barn area. Plant the young box (*Buxus sempervirens*) cutting to make a tree.

To make the barn roof, tie together five pairs of sturdy willow pieces and weave more malleable willow between the sticks. This can be a bit tricky for one person, so two pairs of hands is best.

Cut off the ends to neaten and use garden twine to hold the sides together. Attach the roof to the walls, again using garden twine.

For two pig pens, cut an old plastic flowerpot in half (an adult should do this as cut plastic has sharp edges).

Make pigs by using the dried opium poppy seed heads. Cut off the top of one seed head and place the bottom of another one into the hole: the perfect pig, complete with a cute little pig snout!

Cut four small bits of willow to make legs. Carefully make four holes in the bottom of the 'body' and insert each leg (an adult can use the tip of a sharp knife).

Position your pigs in the muddy compost area, or peeping out of one of the pig pens, and fill your pond with water.

Make sure you keep the turf and box tree watered

Enjoy your miniature farm

If no seed heads are available, the farm could make a perfect setting for plastic animals.

Fairy garden

AGE RANGE **Four years onwards**

TIME OF YEAR **Summer–autumn**

Plastic seed tray

Compost

Low growing plants, such as small rock plants (we used *Raoulia haastii*, an evergreen, mat-forming perennial that looks like grass)

Few flower stems for a fairy tree (we used some stems of smoke bush (*Cotinus coggygria*) and grape hyacinth (*Muscari armeniacum*)

Garden twine

Seeds heads for a fairy castle (we cut off the seed heads of the bulb *Nectaroscordum siculum* subsp *bulgaricum* and also used *Clematis tangutica*)

Shell or half a walnut for a fairy pool

Selection of small, summer bedding or rockery plants (we used pink ones because that is Rose's favourite colour!)

Dried seed heads, to decorate the picture

Fairies!

Fairies and nature go together like beans on toast (Harry's favourite meal!). It is said that fairies will most likely reveal themselves to children whose innocence will not scare them, and, as a child, I felt their presence among the flowers and trees of my parents' garden. I never actually saw one, but I have since met a small number of people who have, and I still keep an eye out for them in our garden!

Children love to make miniature gardens, they're easy to put together and stimulate the imagination.

When filling out your fairy garden, plant some pretty low-growing, small-leaved flowers, such as busy Lizzies (*Impatiens*). Go to your local garden centre and choose from the many rock plants that are available – these have miniature leaves and flowers, which are just perfect for a miniature world. When we had finished making our fairy garden, we completed it by adding our own very special fairies, which were given to me by someone who has seen the real ones!

Half fill your seed tray with some compost.

Plant a **low growing** rock plant that looks just like a freshly mown lawn, such as *Raoulia haastii*.

To make a tree, bind together some flower stems with garden twine and stand in the compost, firming in place.

For a fairy castle, stand some seed heads in the compost in the same way.

For a **lovely fairy pool,** use an upturned shell filled with water. For more miniature trees around the pool we used the pretty dried seed heads of grape hyacinth.

Plant your bedding or rockery plants and add any flower heads that you find around the garden.

Water gently and add any of your own fairies.

Dinosaur garden

AGE RANGE **Four years onwards**

TIME OF YEAR **Summer–autumn**

A big container (we used a big trough we already had in the garden, but any large container will do)

Crocks

Compost

Sand

Gravel

Rocks, shells and interesting stones

Selection of different shades of evergreen plants, including ferns and rock plants such as *Sempervivum* and *Sedum*

Your favourite waterproof dinosaurs

Tufa rock

In our dinosaur garden we added a piece of tufa rock, which is a porous limestone that absorbs and retains moisture. It makes ideal conditions for many rock plants, such as this established evergreen, creeping sedum.

It seems that everywhere you turn you'll see a dinosaur image somewhere either smiling at you from a yoghurt pot or advertising a new chocolate breakfast cereal. Our fascination for these enigmatic creatures never seems to diminish.

The Mesozoic age is divided into three periods from the earliest Triassic period through to the Jurassic and finally the Cretaceous period, which is when the dinosaurs finally disappeared 65 million years ago. For much of the dinosaur age there were no flowering plants; they only appeared during the last days of the dinosaur, so for our garden we have only used plants in shades of green for a really authentic looking dinosaur landscape.

Place crocks

on the bottom of the container for drainage and fill up the container with a compost and sand/gravel mix.

Add rocks,

shells and other interesting stones.

Position the plants,

still in their pots, in the container. It is always a good idea to see where they look best before planting them and then changing your mind! We chose to plant Himalayan maidenhair fern (*Adiantum vunustum*), *Asplenium scolopendrium* 'Crispum', lungwort (*Pulmonaria* 'Lewis Palmer') and *Equisetum hyemale*.

Carefully tap

the bottom of each container, then tip with one hand as the other hand gently eases out the plant.

Plant up

your container, taking care to firm the soil around the plants.

Water well.

Add your **favourite dinosaurs** and – hey presto! – you have dinoland!

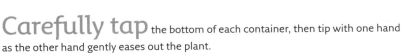

Wormery

AGE RANGE	**Six years onwards**
TIME OF YEAR	**Autumn**

Large glass container with lid with air holes (we used a special wormery kit but large glass jars or vases would do so long as they aren't too wide)
Gravel or small stones for drainage
Garden soil
Fine sand
Vegetable peelings
Garden leaves
Worms from the garden
Dark paper

Worms have been conditioning our planet's soil for millions of years, processing plant waste, aerating the soil and producing fertiliser. Charles Darwin studied worms for many years and concluded that life on earth would not be possible without them, so not only should they be known as the gardener's best friend, but also mankind's!

This project will introduce your children to the concept of recycling while showing them how worms turn organic matter into fertile soil. Always ensure that the contents of the container are moist, but not too wet or dry as worms breathe through their skin, which must remain moist to absorb oxygen from the air. The project should only last for a few weeks, after which the worms should be returned to the garden.

Add coarse drainage to the

bottom of the container to prevent it from becoming waterlogged, which would suffocate the worms. This could be gravel or small stones.

Add a layer of garden soil and then add a layer of sand.

Continue **adding layers** of sand and soil until the container is about three-quarters full. These layers will help you to see how the worms move around and dig tunnels.

Add vegetable peelings, such

as carrot and potato, and garden leaves for the worms to feed on.

Find worms from the garden. Carefully add them to the wormery and watch them wriggle through.

Worms

Try to observe your wormery only in dimly lit conditions and always remember to replace the dark covers when you are not studying the worms.

Through the sides of your wormery you will see worms eating their way through the soil to produce burrows, digesting food from the surface when you feed them and dragging some down into the burrows.

There are two main types of worm, surface and deep litter worms. Lob worms (or nightcrawlers) are deep litter worms and live in the ground about 3m (10ft) deep. They burrow up to the surface at night to eat and breed, leaving their castings (a very concentrated fertiliser) on the surface of the soil. Warm, damp evenings are the best time to go in search of them, or a piece of carpet placed on a patio near grass will attract them if it's kept moist and some earth is sprinkled beneath.

Place **dark paper** around the container to prevent light from entering, and put a secure lid with air holes on top.

Store the container somewhere cool and dark. This will stimulate the worms to tunnel and mix up the layers.

Remember to add organic **food scraps** as the need arises. Holly and Luke tried different fruit, vegetables, paper, bread and cereals to see if they could tell which type of food their worms preferred.

Bird cake

AGE RANGE **Four years onwards**

TIME OF YEAR **Autumn**

Shredded suet, however much suet you are using, combine with an equal amount of the following ingredients:

Bird seed mix

Sunflower seeds

Fresh peanuts

Breadcrumbs

Dried fruit, chopped and soaked to prevent it expanding in the birds' stomachs

Empty onion bag or bird feeder

During winter, when natural food resources, such as insects, worms, berries and seeds, are scarce, garden birds become increasingly dependent on us to supplement their diets. Making a bird feeder will encourage birds into the garden, affording us closer inspection of our feathered friends, perhaps even photographing them. Almost any kitchen leftovers are suitable for garden birds, but it is not a good idea to put out loose whole peanuts in spring and summer as a whole peanut fed to a baby bird might choke it. Don't forget that birds will also appreciate a shallow bowl of water to drink and bathe in.

Mix together all the ingredients except for the suet.

Pour the shredded suet into a saucepan and melt over a gentle heat – always have an adult to hand for this part of the project.

Pour the melted suet (again, an adult job) into a glass bowl.

Add the **remaining ingredients** and stir together with a wooden spoon. Leave for about 30 minutes until it is cool enough to handle.

Take handfuls of the mixture and form into small balls.

Drop the balls into the empty onion bag or your feeder. Squish it all together to make a big sausage.

Tie the end with string and hang in a tree.

Bird food

Other foods to leave out for the birds include:

Bread crumbled up, wholemeal is best (soak it first)

Cooked potatoes, rice and pasta

Stale biscuits and cake

Fruit (dried fruit must always be soaked)

Bacon rind, fat trimmed from meat (make sure both are cut up into small pieces) and suet

Peanuts in wire mesh containers or peanuts in their shells threaded through with string using a darning needle (never use salted peanuts as these can cause birds to dehydrate)

Fresh coconut (saw in half and hang outside – a job for an adult)

Never feed highly spiced food, salted nuts, dried coconut (it swells inside their stomachs) or fruit to garden birds, and always soak dried bread.

Woven nature frame

AGE RANGE	**Six years onwards**
TIME OF YEAR	**Autumn**

Four lengths of bamboo or sturdy sticks from the garden
Strong garden twine
Collection of garden 'finds'

Helping children to look at nature in different ways can only enhance their appreciation of it. Elevating a humble snail's shell or a feather to a work of art will open children's minds to all the natural beauty around them. I collect natural objects throughout the year, such as feathers, snail shells or seed heads, and keep them in the shed for craft projects such as this. But be prepared to take a few deep breaths as coveted *Allium* heads and other favourite flowers are proudly presented to you woven through the frame ... the children are only doing what the inspired natural artist Andy Goldsworthy has made his fortune from!

Bind the corners of the frame using the twine, making sure you tie the knots very tightly as the frame will need to be sturdy.

Wind string across the frame in one direction and then the other, to create a string mesh.

Weave in **feathers ...**

lavender ...

dried flower heads and ...

snail shells, which Bryony and I gently pierced and attached with string. Of course, you can weave anything else you find in the garden.

Tie and cut off any surplus string, then tie a long length of ribbon or twine to the ends, so you can hang up your natural woven collage.

Christmas wreath

AGE RANGE **Eight years onwards**

TIME OF YEAR **Winter**

Pliable stems from shrubs including climbers such as hazel, wisteria, honeysuckle, or a grape vine can be used, as well as willow stems

Garden twine

Pine cones

Paint (children's or left-over emulsion)

Small paintbrushes

Dried poppy seed heads with stems

Ribbons, we used gold and silver

Glitter

Glue

Other ideas

Of course, wreaths don't have to be just for Christmas. You could add paint to dried wreaths like this one, and add hearts and flowers to make a unique wedding present.

I love everything about Christmas, mince pies, sparkling fairy lights and watching *The Snowman* (that's me by the way, not Harry and Rose!). I've made quite a few decorations over the years, and Hal and I always design and print our own cards, even when time is tight (which it always is). I really enjoy decorating the house for the festive season, and it is lovely to reacquaint myself with cherished decorations from years gone by, but I always like to introduce a few new ones.

Our Christmas wreath is really easy to make and, of course, considerably cheaper than ones you buy. We used mostly natural objects found either in the garden or collected on walks, which I keep in the shed throughout the year, as well as some ribbon kept from last year's presents and the children's paints. Young children can paint the cones and poppy seed heads, while older ones can plait and tie the plant stems.

Strip the leaves off three long plant stems and then tie them together (each about 1m (1yd) at one end). Plait them together fairly tightly.

Carefully bend the plaited stems to form a circle and tie firmly with garden twine.

Tie twine around the base of some pine cones and attach them at regular intervals around the wreath.

Paint the tips of the cones with white paint to look like a dusting of snow. You could then sprinkle glitter onto the pine cones to add some sparkle.

Paint the dried poppy seed heads. We pushed ours into Rose's Play Dough until they dried.

When the poppy heads have dried, weave the stems into the wreath.

Add bows and ribbons and hang on the front door for a cheerful festive welcome.

Christmas tree

AGE RANGE **Eight years onwards**

TIME OF YEAR **Winter**

Fairly straight sticks collected from the garden (we used some dried willow stems, but thin bamboo could also be used)

Strong garden twine

Log base

Drill

Paint (children's or left-over emulsion)

Paintbrush

Thin garden wire

Pine cones

Dried poppy seed heads

Glue

Glitter, optional

Thin string, to tie poppy seed heads onto the tree

I made one of these for Harry's first Christmas using vines and sticks that I found in the garden. There is something very satisfying about creating your own Christmas decorations, especially if all you have to do is go out into the garden to fetch the raw materials. It saves lots of money, too! We've used dried poppy seed heads and pine cones to decorate our tree. Keep an eye out for potential material to work with when you're out in the garden or going for a walk – for instance, dried rose hips, safe berries or walnut. You never know when they might come in useful.

Cut willow stems or sticks

to length. Our uprights are 60cm (24in) long and the bottom stick of each triangle is about 50cm (20in), 40cm (16in) and 30cm (12in) long.

Before you go any further, lay out the design to ensure that all the sticks fit together well.

Bind the corners of each of the three smaller triangles using strong garden twine, which gives the knots extra strength.

Drill two holes into a log base (an adult job) and insert the two longer stems. This forms the base triangle on which to tie the three smaller triangles. To make the tall triangular shape, bind the stems together at the top.

Tie each of the three smaller triangles onto the basic frame.

Paint the tree a single colour or use different ones for each of the triangles. When the paint has dried, use garden wire to attach the pine cones. Wrap a piece of wire around the lowest 'branches' of each cone, twist firmly and then attach the other end of the wire to the tree.

Paint the tips of the cones white to look like a light covering of snow (you could also use glitter).

Make a willow star (see page 46), and paint it white to put on the top of the Christmas tree.

Tie string around the **dried opium poppy heads,** which make perfect Christmas baubles once painted. When dry, tie them to the tree.

PLANT DIRECTORY

The plants I've chosen for this directory are by no means an exhaustive list, but ones that I've either enjoyed growing myself or admired from afar! Seed catalogues list a treasure trove of goodies, and make interesting reading during the winter months, but if you haven't the time, many garden centres now carry a good range of children's easy-to-grow seed packets, which should get them started.

Easy-grow flowering annuals

SS = flowers that self-seed, which makes them truly excellent value
See also Rose's rainbow (page 34)

Calendula officinalis (pot marigold) (SS)
Centaurea cyanus (cornflower) (SS)
Convolvulus tricolour (dwarf morning glory)
Cosmos bipinnatus (SS)
Gypsophila elegans (baby's breath) (SS)
Helianthus annuus (sunflower) (SS)
Helichrysum bracteatum (strawflower)
Iberis umbellata (candytuft) (SS)
Limnanthes douglasii
Linum rubrum (scarlet flax)
Myosotis (forget-me-not)(SS)
Nigella damascena (love-in-a-mist) (SS)
Papaver (poppy) (SS)
Tropaeolum majus (nasturtium) (SS)
Viola (pansy)
Zinnia

Fragrant and aromatic plants

See also Sensory garden – smell (page 91)

Agastache foeniculum (anise hyssop)
Akebia quinata (chocolate vine)
Aloysia triphylla (lemon-scented verbena)
Azara microphylla.
Cercidiphyllum japonicum (katsura tree)
Chamaemelum nobile 'Treneague'
Clematis montana 'Elizabeth'
Cosmos atrosanguineus (chocolate cosmos)
Cytisus battandieri (pineapple broom)

Galium odoratum (woodruff)
Helichrysum angustifolium (curry plant)
Jasminum officinale (jasmine)
Lavandula stoechas subsp. *pedunculata* (papillon or butterfly lavender)
Lonicera periclymenum (honeysuckle)
Lonicera x purpusii (winter honeysuckle)
Melianthus major (honey bush)
Philadelphus 'Silberregen'
Salvia elegans (pineapple sage)
Thymus (thyme)
Trachelospermum jasminoides (star jasmine)
Viola odorata (sweet violets)
Wisteria

Cosmos atrosanguineus

Herbaceous plants for awe-inspiring height

See also Sunflower bed (page 26) and Sensory garden – sight (page 92)

Allium giganteum
Angelica archangelica (angelica)
Crambe cordifolia
Cynara cardunculus (cardoon)
Ferula communis (giant fennel)
Gunnera manicata (giant rhubarb)
Helianthus annuus (sunflower)
Nectaroscordum siculum subsp. *bulgaricum*
Onopordum acanthium (Scotch thistle)
Rheum palmatum 'Atrosanguineum' (ornamental rhubarb)
Rudbeckia 'Herbstonne'

Gunnera manicata

Plants that attract wildlife

Nectar-rich butterfly favourites:

Aster x frikartii (Michaelmas daisy)
Aubrieta (aubretia)
Buddleja davidii (butterfly bush)
Centranthus ruber (red valerian)
Chrysanthemum leucanthemum (oxeye daisy)
Cytisus (broom)
Echinacea purpurea (coneflower)

Echinacea purpurea 'Alba'

Eryngium x *tripartitum*
Galanthus nivalis (snowdrop)
Hebe (hebe)
Hyacinthoides non-scripta (bluebell)
Knautia macedonica

Knautia macedonica

Lavandula (lavender)
Lonicera periclymenum (honeysuckle)
Narcissus pseudonarcissus (lent lily)
Nepeta (catmint)
Primula vulgaris (primrose)
Sedum 'Herbstfreude' (ice plant)

Syringa (lilac)
Thymus (thyme)
Verbena bonariensis

Verbena bonariensis

Plants to attract birds:

Choisya ternata (Mexican orange blossom)
Cynara cardunculus (cardoon)
Echinops ritro (globe thistle)

Echinops ritro

Hedera (ivy)
Helianthus annuus (sunflower)
Ilex (holly)
Lonicera periclymenum (woodbine)
Pyracantha 'Navaho' (firethorn)
Rosa glauca
Rosa rugosa

Nectar-rich plants to attract bees:

Agastache
Anemone blanda (as well as other early flowering bulbs)

Aster (Michaelmas daisy)
Aubrieta (aubretia)
Buddleja davidii (butterfly bush)
Caryopteris
Echinacea (coneflower)
Echinops ritro (globe thistle)
Erysimum (wallflower)
Hebe (hebe)
Knautia macedonica
Lavandula (lavender)
Limnanthes douglasii (poached egg flower)

Limnanthes douglasii

Mentha (mint)
Nepeta (catmint)
Origanum (oregano)
Rosmarinus (rosemary)
Salvia (sage)
Scabiosa (scabious)
Skimmia (skimmia)

Small native trees to attract wildlife:

Betula pendula (silver birch)
Crataegus persimilis 'Prunifolia' (hawthorn)
Malus sargentii (flowering crab apple)
Prunus 'Amanogawa' (Lombardy cherry)
Sorbus aucuparia (mountain ash)

Interesting edible plants

See also Sensory garden – taste (page 94) and various other projects throughout the book.

Courgettes: 'Ambassador F1', 'Leprechaun' and 'Bambino F1'

Cucumbers: 'Crystal Lemon'

Kidney beans: 'Black and White'

Monkey nuts

Peas: 'Feltham First', 'Meteor' and 'Douce Provence', which can be sown directly into the ground. Varieties suitable for sowing from early spring to summer include: 'Kelvedon Wonder', 'Hurst Green Shaft' and 'Sugar Snap'.

Pumpkins: 'Jack-O-Lantern' and, for big pumpkins, 'Atlantic Giant'

Strawberries: early mid-summer varieties (fruiting from June to early July): 'Honeoye', 'Elvira', 'Rosie'; mid-summer varieties (fruiting through July): 'Elsanta', 'Cambridge Favourite', 'Pegasus'; late summer varieties (mid-July to early August): 'Florence', 'Alice', 'Maxim'; perpetual varieties include: 'Mara des Bois', 'Vivarosa', 'Challenger'.

Sweetcorn: 'Strawberry Popcorn'

Tomatoes: 'Moneymaker', 'Gardener's Delight' and 'Tumbling Tom Red'/'Tumbling Tom Yellow'. 'Tomatillo' look like green tomatoes, but are enclosed in a silk-like skin and taste sweet.

Wild or Alpine strawberries (*Fragaria vesca*)

Tactile plants

See also Sensory Garden – touch (page 95).

Allium hollandicum 'Purple Sensation'

Allium hollandicum

Ballota pseudodictamnus

Bassia scoparia f. *trichophylla* (burning bush)

Bracteantha bracteata (strawflower)
Colourful annual that is very tactile.

Foeniculum vulgare purpureum (fennel)

Helianthus 'Teddy Bear'

Helichrysum bracteatum (strawflower)

Lagurus ovatus (hare's tail)

Lavandula stoechas subsp. *pedunculata* (papillon or butterfly lavender)

Lychnis coronaria (rose campion)

Papaver orientale (Oriental poppy)

Pennisetum alopecuroides (fountain grass)

Pennisetum alopecuroides

Phlomis russeliana

Potentilla atrosanguinea

Pulsatilla vulgaris (pasqueflower)

Salix caprea 'Kilmarnock'

Salvia argentea (silver sage)

Senecio cineraria 'Silver Dust'

Stachys byzantina (lambs' ears)

Stachys byzantina

Stipa tenuissima 'Ponytails'

Verbascum bombyciferum (giant silver mullein)

Musical plants

See also Sensory garden – sound (page 93)

Briza media (quaking grass)
Cortaderia selloana (pampas grass)
Lunaria annua (honesty)

Lunaria annua

Miscanthus sinensis 'Silberfeder'
Papaver somniferum (opium poppy)
Phylostachys vivax 'Aureocaulis'
Populus tremula 'Pendula' (weeping aspen)
Stipa gigantea (feather grass)

Moisture loving plants

See also Rose's aquatic garden (page 82) and Harry's bog garden (page 85)

Acorus gramineus 'Ogon' (sweet flag)
Astilbe
Brunnera macrophylla
Caltha palustris (marsh marigold)
Eichhornia crassipes (water hyacinth
Elodea canadensis (Canadian pondweed)
Equisetum fluviatile (horsetail rush)
Gunnera manicata
Hosta
Juncus ensifolius
Ligularia przewalskii
Lobelia cardinalis
Menyanthes trifoliate (bog bean)
Myosotis palustris 'Semperflorens' (forget-me-not)
Myosotis scorpioides (water forget-me-nots)
Nymphaea (water lily)

Oenanthe fistulosa 'Flamingo' (water dropwort)
Osmunda regalis (royal fern)
Phalaris arundinacea var *picta* (gardener's garters)
Primula japonica (candleabra primula)
Rheum palmatum 'Atrosanguineum' (ornamental rhubarb)
Sisyrinchium angustifolium (blue satin flower)
Trollius europaeus (European globeflower)

Trollius europaeus

Bulbs

See also Naturalising bulbs (page 96)

Anemone blanda (winter flowering)
Camassia leichtlinii (quamash) (summer flowering)

Camassia leichtlinii

Colchicum autumnale (naked ladies) (autumn flowering)
Crocus speciosus (autumn crocus) (autumn flowering)

Crocus tommasinianus (winter flowering)
Cyclamen coum (winter flowering)
Cyclamen hederifolium (autumn flowering)
Eranthis hyemalis (winter aconite) (winter flowering)
Galanthus nivalis (snowdrop) (winter flowering)
Gladiolus byzantinus (summer flowering)

Galanthus nivalis

Hyacinthoides non-scripta (bluebells) (spring flowering)
Muscari armeniacum (grape hyacinth) (spring flowering)

Muscari armeniacum

Narcissus 'February Gold' (winter flowering)
Narcissus pseudonarcissus (lent lily) (spring flowering)

ACKNOWLEDGEMENTS

Special thanks go to

Our many models and their 'assistants'; Hal, Rose and Harry; Mason and Mandy; Darcey, Bryony, Nick and Yvette; Holly, Luke, Lynda and Sean; Elliott, Isobel and Cate. Thanks also to Ray Hale for his fabulous building work, Barbara Clift for the beautiful willow creations, Judith Glover for such fantastic illustrations, and Nikki English for her lovely photographs. Finally, thanks also to Richard Lucas, David Fountain, Angela Newton and Luke Griffin.

Suppliers

Bob's Tyres & Exhausts Ltd
Stevenage Old Town
Herts, SG1 3HH

P. H. Coate & Son, Somerset
Tel: 01823 490249
(willow suppliers by mail order)

Cut Price Tiles
33 Wilbury Way
Herts, SG4 0TW

Cuprinol Garden Shades
Available from leading DIY and garden stores or visit
www.cuprinol.co.uk /tel: 01753 550555

David Fountain
Website: www.gardensforkids.com

Fulham Palace Garden Centre
Bishops Avenue, London, SW6
(All profits from the garden centre go to the charity Fairbridge, which supports inner city youth)

Mark Turner & Michael Steel
Website: www.enchanted.co.uk
(fairy suppliers)

Vanstone Park of Codicote
Hitchin Road
Herts, SG4 8TH

Willowpool Designs, Cumbria
Steve & Simone
Tel: 01539 567056

Photographs on pages 52 and 94 by Lynda Brazier

The illustrations in this book were created by Judith Glover
Email: info@judithglover.com
Website: www.judithglover.com

For further advice on using willow contact Barbara Clift
Tel: 01884 266358
Email: barbara@raymentlloyd.co.uk